GUIDE – BOOK

THE CUMBRAES

FIRTH OF CLYDE

INCLUDING CHAPTERS ON

WEMYSS BAY, LARGS AND FAIRLIE

BY

W. LYTTEIL M.A.

AUTHOR OF "LANDMARKS OF SCOTTISH LIFE AND
LANGUAGE."

WITH MAP AND ILLUSTRATIONS

Lytteil, W. Guide-Book To The Cumbraes, Firth Of Clyde, Including Chapters On Wemyss Bay, Largs and Fairlie. 1886. Carlisle. Printed by Halstead & Beaty, City Works, Edinburgh: Menzies & Co.

PUBLISHED BY

CELTIC NEW DAWN PRESS

2016

E-Mail: ceilteachtusnua@gmail.com

GUIDE - BOOK

TO

THE CUMBRAES

FIRTH OF CLYDE

INCLUDING CHAPTERS ON

WEMYSS BAY, LARGS, AND FAIRLIE

BY

W. LYTTEIL, M.A.,

Author of "Landmarks of Scottish Life and Language."

WITH MAP AND ILLUSTRATIONS.

CARLISLE:
PRINTED BY HALSTEAD & BEATY, CITY WORKS,
EDINBURGH: MENZIES & CO.
[Copyright Registered 1886]

PRICE ONE SHILLING

Foreword:

The Isles of Cumbrae on Scotland's west coast are a source of endless inspiration to anyone lucky enough to live on them and a source of great joy to anybody who might visit them.

The natural beauty of 'Great Cumbrae' and its sister island 'Wee Cumbrae' attract tourists by the hundreds in summertime, most of whom enjoy sight-seeing in the larger island's main town of Millport.

Of course, there is much more to these hidden gems of the Inner Hebrides; their histories are as rare and unique as their beautiful landscapes.

The book's author W. Lytteil brought it all to life when he first published this book in 1886; highlighting landmarks, place-names, family names and the lives of those who lived here and shaped the islands' future with both poetic skill and great accuracy.

The guide-book is presented in its original form, aside from a few minor edits. These consist of the addition of paragraph breaks due to the lengthy writing style of the author and a couple of typo corrections. Otherwise the grammar and language used are still fully intact.

There's also little doubt that this manuscript will already exist somewhere out there on the internet and could probably be read on-line for free. However, if you prefer having a physical copy of a book in your hands as I do, then you'll appreciate its modern reprinting. There's something much more satisfying about turning the pages of a real book, compared to reading it from a computer or phone screen.

Anyone visiting the Isles of Cumbrae and the surrounding areas will also be able use it as it was first intended; as a handy guide book to take along with you on your travels, as well as one to keep on your bookshelves at home. The places and landmarks described within have changed little in their wondrous beauty since the author wrote about them.

This book has an even greater value though; as it represents a snapshot in time. The thoughts of the original author W. Lytteil and his knowledge of the history of the isles are captured perfectly. Their timeless quality should further enrich the lives of anyone who might read them.

Lastly, in an ideal world, even the equivalent original price of 'one shilling' should still apply; but the high costs of modern printing simply rule that out. However, production costs have been kept to a minimum, thus so has the selling price.

Therefore, without further ado, it gives me great pleasure to re-introduce this guide book, which was something of a lost treasure, to the public domain once again.

Seán Gearárd McCloskey

[Kames Bay, Isle Of Cumbrae, 2016]

This version of 'Guide-Book to the Cumbraes' is dedicated to all who care about the islands; their landscapes, wildlife and communities.

CONTENTS:

ISLE OF CUMBRAE.

CHAPTER I.

VIEW OF MILLPORT AND ITS SURROUNDINGS.

THERE are few watering-places in the Firth of Clyde which have proved more winsome and attractive than Millport, in the Isle of Cumbrae. As the visitor from Largs or Fairlie approaches the pier by steamboat, he finds himself in the bossom of a deep sunny bay, which faces the south and delights the eye with a beautiful picture of green engirdling hills and lofty red cliffs.

The general features of the scene are singularly pleasing and varied. Within the two wing-like promontories which, on east and west, enfold the waters of the bay, lie a number of sheltering rock-islets; and the innermost shore-line presents a beautiful arrangement of fine bathing sands, which are separated or intersected by picturesque dispositions of rock.

The houses of the village hug the shore, --every one as radiant as summer sunshine and beautiful white stone can make it. The more recently built villas bend round the sinuosities of the bays or adorn the terraced heights; while overall a number of handsome churches crown the scene,

1

imparting beauty and dignity to it by their noble presence.

A sloping background of well-tilled fields and green hills give fine effect to the harmonious blending of all the more salient features of the landscape, and the seas-side portion of the picture presents an animated spectacle of happy juveniles, disporting on the sands or plunging into the clear waters of the briny bath. Seared yachts and yawls are cruising about, and look like lovely sea-birds skimming the main, while a scattered multitude of little boats, filled with happy occupants, are paddling about the bay or moving gaily around the islets. On a fine summer afternoon or evening the scene is superb, and becomes all the more so when the tall red cliffs of the Farland glow like burnished bronze as the western sun throws its full blaze of light upon them.

Farther away, but in fine weather always clearly visible, are the lofty sky-piercing peaks of the two great Goatfells in Arran, the towering horn of Kcervohr and the majestic pike of Greenan Ahval in the same island; Torr-mor and Suy Blane in the south of Bute; Ailsa Craig in the far distance, rising loftily above the waves like a vast conical watch-tower; and Holy Island, or Melansey, near Lamlash. In the nearer foreground, as one looks southward, rises the finely trap-terraces and crag-adorned Isle of Little Cumbrae, or Wee Cumra, its eastern shore guarded by a strong and well-preserved ancient castle. Over against this grim old fortalice, but on a rocky ness or point of the Ayrshire coast, stands a castle of similar age and build--the old castle of Pencorse, or Portcrosch--once the residence of royalty, and long held by a noble ayrshire family of the name of Ross.

Between this castle-crowned promontary and the lofty ridge of the Kaim Hill above Fairlie, a landscape of unrivalled beauty unfolds itself to the eye of the observer, and is daily seen, as from the most favourable view-point, from the shores of Cumbrae. To the left or east of the old weather-word castle on the point there is a prominent hill crowned with a vitrified fort, and designated Auld-hill--a probable contraction for Aulbury-hill. A little farther to the left, as the coast tends northwards, the eye rests upon the lofty and picturesque cliffs of Ardneil--a name which signifies the hill or promontory of the precipice. Following in the same direction we have next a fine view of the beautiful hills and tree-clad slopes of Goldenberry, or Goudenbury--a Norse compound denoting the heroes' camp.

HUNTERSTON HOUSE--stands on the lower grounds of the King's hunters--stands on the lower grounds which form its own proper demesne, and looks out upon the waters of the firth from its green environment of woods. Paltreath is its ancient name, and the fact becomes the more interesting when we see that it signifies the chieftain's residence. The green hills in the distance, to the back of Hunterston, lie along the eastern side of the parish of West Kilbride.

Caldron-gattel is the name of one of the summits, and signifies the burying-place of the Celtic chiefs--the cairns being still intact. It is well seen over the Red Farland crag as one stands on the eastern slope of Trahoun-hill, near the public school. Kaim Hill is the much higher ridge, which is seen farther to the left, its height being 1270 feet. St. Annan's chapel site and the charming village of Fairlie lie at the foot of its green slopes, but are not visible from the station at Trahoun.

CHAPTER II.
LOCAL DETAILS AND DESCRIPTIONS

(I.) FROM THE PIER TO THE LORNE.

LANDING on the pier and looking towards the west, one cannot but admire the fine green promontory called The Lorne. It is the terminal portion of the copse-clad braes or slopes which, in that quarter, form such a fine natural crescent, and shelter so effectually the western villas. It overlooks, too, the low rocky point called Portahar Point, which forms the south-western extremity of the island. As a name it has a similar origin to that of Lorn in Argyll, being a Gaelic term denoting the site of a ruined fort. In the case of the Cumbrae Lorne the foundations, fosse, and other vestiges of a ruined strength were, about fourteen years ago , discovered on its site by the writer, and the discovery has since been amply confirmed by competent judges.

The reality of the site has been strengthened to a degree by other interesting facts and associations. One of these may be mentioned here, although the subject is one that will come up again in connection with the very ancient ecclesiastical site in the vicinity-at Kirktoun. The fact referred to is the name of Kennara Borough, a name which to this day clings to the land immediately adjacent to the Lorne, and inclusive of the ancient site itself. Now, the name of Kennara Borough is clearly a Norse appellation, and as clearly and certainly it signifies the Preceptors' burg or stronghold, in other words, the fortified station of the learned churchmen. It points to the time-more than a thousand years ago-when the fierce Vikingar, or sea-rovers of the North, swept down like hunger-driven hawks upon the little Christian community which gathered round their pastors and teachers in the neighbouring Kirk-toun of Cumbrae. The necessity for a place of refuge or defence would be at once perceived, especially if any swift post from Iona had hastened through with news of the fell havoc wrought there by the heathen marauders.

Accordingly, and without delay, a place of defence would be planned. With heart and hand the accomplished clerics and their lay associates would pursue the work, and in due time a goodly and substantial structure would reward their labours. If it proved, in the trial, insufficient for their protection, their fate would be only as the fate of the holders of not a few much stronger bulwarks since.

Certain it is that the Norsemen speedily acquired complete mastery over these islands. In some cases they owed their conquests entirely to the sword, and in other cases by alliances with native families of position. The ruinous and destructive character of their earlier assaults upon the Christianised populations of the West made their baneful deeds severely felt by the churches; and in not a few instances shepherd and flock were, in one fell swoop, cut off,-their "holy and beautiful" houses overthrown, and the happy fruits of righteousness and of an advancing civilization obliterated. But only for a season were these things to be-a brief season in some places, a longer one in others. The cup of affliction was drained, the uplifted scourge was arrested in its descent. Warrior chiefs buried the hatchet and made the surviving Christians welcome to return to their desolated shrines. Grim old believers in Thor and Woden succumbed to the blessed spirit of the Gospel and renounced their freets and superstitions.

In the first ardour of their new faith they warmly espoused the cause of the Christians, and hastened to build up the churches which once they destroyed. Scattered stragglers who had escaped from the first fury of the invaders would timidly return to their homes, and assist in re-building the ruined fanes. So it may have been with the survivors of the Cumbrae community who had worshipped God in the Keill or Church which stood within the walls of the existing cemetery at Kirkton.

Not a few remembrances of this very ancient church remain to this day. Keill-well, and Kilmethe, as local names referring to the sacred edifice, are still in daily use. We have also six beautiful crosses and sundry sculptured stones beside-all evidently of the eighth or ninth century period-which have been dug out of the hallowed ground of the old churchyard; and, further, we have, in the Aberdeen Breviary, a most interesting account of the two godly companions, Beya and Maura, whose lengthened labours as Christian lady Missionaries and zenana workers in the West have been amply verified.

Besides these precious relics and remembrances of the ecclesiastical past in these islands we have sundry others, a full account of which must be reserved for another section. It may here, however, be stated that the name of

CUMBRAE

"The Cimbraes" [kim'raes] has evidently its true origin in the Kimmora or Keil-Maura, a compound name which signifies the church of Maura. According to this view, or conclusion, the full name of the island would be InchKeilMaura, that is, the island of the church (dedicated to the memory) of Maura. So also with the Little or "Wee" Cumbrae: it is the island of Chapel Santa Vey,-in other words, the island of the Chapel of St. Beya.

8

Ere leaving the steamboat pier the interested visitor may observe Knox's Port on the west side of it,-a narrow creek or "goe" which runs up between high rocks and penetrates a considerable way inland. Here passengers landed in wherries or small boats from the steamers prior to the building of the pier, and high up on the Rock-heads, immediately to the west of the fine natural inlet, stood, in old times, the strong house or "peel" called the Sheriff's Auld Ha'. This was the Hall or mansion of the Sheriff of Bute, who, as lord of the manor, seems to have occasionally made it his residence, or used it as a lodge when he desired to have a few day's shooting or hunting. The "Sheriff" was the Stewart of Bute, whose representative to-day is the Most Noble the Marquis of Bute. His jurisdiction in old times extended over his lands and dependants in both islands, and included the feudal privilege of deciding causes, or passing sentence on evildoers.

The Old Harbour is at the head of the steamboat pier, and was, about the middle of the last century, excavated from the solid white sandstone rock,-the great slabs or blocks of stone having been quarried on behalf of the Government in order to supply building materials for use in the construction of the harbour of Portpatrick, in Galloway.

As the stream called the Millburn ran down the slope of what is now Cardiff street into the sea at this spot, it naturally came about that the residents on the island designated this newly-formed harbour "the Millport,"-so distinguishing it from the Foule-port on the west, and from Portloy on the Farland-side. Millburn House stands stands near the site of the old cornmill, and Millbrae is the upper portion of Cardiff-street.

From a geological point of view this section of the coast-line must have been very remarkable. Immediately south of the then site of the present old harbour rose an elevated boss, or somewhat rounded mass of rock which, called Craiglee, or the hoary crag, became completely insulated by the periodical influx of the tide; and, strange to relate, there stood upon this swelling rocky eminence what the old people of the last generation used to call a Changehouse.

This was the tavern of the locality, to which some of the strong-armed quarrymen might at times resort and discuss the news of the day over a pot of ale. Could fancy prevail to fill up the picture and describe the accessories of this primitive alehouse, we might find it a rival to Goldsmith's wayside inn. Were sailors' trophies there, "wisely kept for show" upon the aumrie shelf or adorning the mantelpiece, shells from the Orient of many a pearly hue, a dried flying-fish that seemed to have just alighted on the top of a brass candlestick, and a great black-beetle or scarabaeus resting on its fellow at the other end of the shelf; while between the two last-named did there not stand a pair of fine walrus tusks, the tips of which came into contact and formed a high pointed arch over a lovely rose-coloured tuft of West Indian coral?

What a sensation on a winter's night would a right strong gale from the south-west create among the inmates and frequenters of this doubly insular howff! Every thud of the huge thundering billows which flung themselves bodily upon the rock and made it almost tremble at the shock, would carry a message of awe to the hearts of the inmates and thrill their whole inner man with a solemn sense of the grandeur of the might of Him who rides in the whirlwind and riles in the storm. And when the gathering tempest had reached its climax and spent itself in a last passionate outburst, what a sight it would be to see the rolling cloudlegions of the sky disperse themselves and give place to the empire of the fair arbitress of night, whose silvery splendour caught each dashing billow as it shot up wildly into the air, and transformed the highflying shower of meteoric spray into a veil of snowwhite and pearly lustre.

As an opposite experience to that of a storm, let the visitor on a fine summer day, when the tide is near its lowest ebb, find his way down to Knox's Port by turning from the harbour to the left, and passing through an opening in the nearer end of Clydestreet. Here the white freestone of the locality may be seen in contact with a huge erupted mass of dark volcanic rock, and so completely altered into a stone of almost flinty hardness as to be scarcely recognisable.

The port itself is thought to have received its name from one of the early visitors to this charming seaside resort, but it is highly probable that our little creek or inlet had its own proper name long before James Knox, chemist, caused the steps to be cut in the rock. About sixty-five yards to the west of this convenient landing place for small boats, a number of "pots" or cavities in the hard rock may be seen. They are remarkable examples of the grinding power of the waves, especially when a "kobble" or small boulder is found acting like a pestle at the bottom of the pot. The exact or precise spot is marked by a skerry or rugged ledge of rocks running into the sea at right angles to the line of the rockbound coast, and the name of Bessyport attaches itself to the locality.

Whether "port" or whether the word "buss," signifying a rock or skerry which the sea overflows, applies here, it were hard perhaps to decide. Such skerries are called "busks" by the fisherfolk at Bullers o' Buchan, and a similar skerry lying off Eyemouth harbour bears the name of Bushcraig. In the latter instance the word "craig" has recently superseded a much older portion of the name, for the appellation of name of the skerry was originally Boeskerry, meaning the rock of boding or warning breakers. It has only to be added here that the general name for this rockbound portion of our islandshore is Rockheads.

LeaddyMary is about one hundred and sixty yards to the westward, and gives name to a huge peaked boulder which stands in the water near the mouth of the small seainlet called Wee Fouleport.

FOULE PORT.

The next sea inlet to the west is a much larger one, and penetrates about twice as far into the land. Fouleport is the name by which it has been known time out of mind, but it is pretty certain that the name does not seem to find favour in these days of aesthetic culture, and on all hands we now hear it called West Bay. If the innovation were to end here an act of toleration might be passed-a Briton's right to growl beforehand being conceded-but the tyrant Fashion does not get an

13

inch but she wants an ell, and so the beautiful name of Kames Bay must likewise be consigned to oblivion and supplanted by the inane appellation of East Bay. It is admitted that the words "East" and "West" are handy monosyllables, and worthy in every way to fill respectively a vacant post; but where the "situation" is already filled up proper names of character deserve the unchallenged respect which is universally and ungrudgingly given to all good public servants.

By all means, then let Fouleport remain as the honoured name which has nobly served the Cumbrae public for generations. Whatever be its real name or original signification, we may rest assured that it had at the first a character of specific appropriateness which puts the epithet "west" into the category of vaguest generalities.

The following excerpt from a previous work has reference to the philology of the name of Fouleport:-

" There is a port or little haven of this name in Bute, and which is also called Portathaiche, that is, giantwarriors' port. This shows that "foul [fool] port" is simply a version of Portnafue, that is, the port of the foes or giantwarriors-port nam fuath. The Foule causeway, near Ayr, means the causeway; and Thirlwall signifies Titans' rampart giants' barrier. Our Fouleport is, therefore, equivalent to port nan athaiche, the port if the mighty warriors, and possibly refers to the Northmen. A huge dyke of great boulders stretched across the bight, but these have been carried off and used as materials for the building of the new pier. Several great slabs of stone, apparently gravestones, were found at the bleach-green near the Teawell in this quarter. The Danish val means a battlefield, and v sometimes becomes f. Faill signifies a cliff, but I do not think either of the two last suggestions can be entertained."-Landmarks, p. 70.

The massive cliffs of white sandstone which protect the eastern side of this seainlet are worthy of careful inspection. They form quite a little promontory of rugged and picturesque character, and afford a good station or vantage-ground for viewing the surrounding scenery. Looking forwards and along the shore, one may observe the prominent rock, or rugged seacliff, called the Hiddockcraig, or the rock of the hooded crow; and, beyond it, the Nethertonrock and Knupkurr. The last of these local names signifies the rugged rockhillock,-cnap garbh. The southernmost rockislet lying off the shore (about five hundred yards distant) is called

THE CLACH,

meaning a stone-the nearest to the spectator is the Leuach (an laogh, the calf), -and the bigger one a little farther to the southeast is named the Spoig, meaning the hamshaped rock. The two other and much larger rocky islets to the east are called

THE ALLENS,

that is, the islands-Gaelic ailiun or eilean, an island, an islet. Homie or Holmie is a very small rockislet, or skerry in the sea, at the back of the two Allens, and it has its name from a Norse term denoting an islet. It appears above water only after five hours of ebb, and it has long been held to be a firstrate place for lythefishing.

Turning the eye landwards and right west, one has from this point of view a beautiful prospect of green slopes, wooded braes, and handsome villas. Big-Brae is the name of the copseclad slopes which are nearer to the Lorne, and Wee Brae lies or slopes away to the north of these. The tilled land at the foot of these "braes" or slopes is called Garbrough-properly Gartbrough,-that is, the cornland of the burg or fortress, and so referring to the ruined fortlet of Kennara Borough or the Lorne. Upon the cultivated land just mentioned there has recently been erected a number of handsome villas, and every one of them occupies a site of undisturbed amenity. The lofty braes on the west, backed by Airdhill, provide a most effective shelter from the stronger westerly winds which, at times, visit our coast. Indeed, the amenity of the climate in this quarter of the island, and the genial warmth which the morning sun pours into it, are both fully proved by the rich, or rather, the exuberant natural growth of the trees, flowers, and bushes which adorn these braes.

Each returning springtime clothes these

BRAES O' LORNE

(as they may fitly be named) with a glory of bloom and foliage which is simply magnificent. The various indigenous sallows, or willowgreen tassels, the hazels show their lovely tufts of olivegreen tassels, the hazels show their sobertinted bloom, the hawthorntrees makes a rich and charming display of snowy blossoms tinged with pink, and the black sloethorns crown their thorny twigs with a perfect effulgence of milkwhite flowers. Ferns and wild flowers in astonishing numbers peep out everywhere among the trees and bushes,-the early or "ratheprimrose" in matchless abundance, the little celandine in its vesture of gold, the wild hyacinth with its pendulous spikes of lovely blue, and the field daisy in countless tufts of "crimson-tippet" flowers.

(2) TOUR ROUND THE ISLAND

A few preliminary directions and details may be here given to those few who have only a few hours to spend on the island. If any such desire to make the best of their brief opportunity, let them enter a brake or hire a wheeled vehicle, and take a drive round the whole of Big Cumbrae. Those who prefer the "marrow-bone stage," should turn eastwards from the pier-head, pass along in front of the Garrison, and hold on their way until they reach the beautiful sandy shore of Kames Bay. Here the road divides, one branch going straight forward along the foot of the well-wooded Innean-brae (een-yan), and onwards towards the north, passing on the left the farmhouse of Ballykellet. The other branch of the road keeps by the seashore, winds round the horse-shoe bay of Kames, then passes right south for nearly half a mile.

Turning the magnificent Red Crags of the Farland, or Foreland, the pedestrian has now a full view of one of the most astonishing of natural monuments, Heatheren Keipel Dyke (heth'ren caple) is the old and time-honoured name by which it is called, and it will at once be seen that this remarkable geological phenomenon starts directly from the plain, and rises up to a great height in the form of a vast cyclopean 'dyke' or wall. Its fellow lifts its lion-like head and shoulders only one-third of a mile ahead, and may, therefore, be reached in five or six minutes. Houllon Keipel Dyke (hollon caple) is the old and interesting name by which this-the more easterly of these two great natural dykes-is known. No other name than this did it have fifty years ago, except the occasional appellation of Deil's Dyke,-a name which may be held to summarise and embody in one personage the host of ogres or fabulous demon-giants which are credited, in an ancient folk's-tale, with the building of this grim-looking structure.

According to the ancient legend or chapter of folk-lore, the stupendous wall of Heatheren Keipel was successfully built up to its present height by the fairies, or good elves, who are to be regarded as the modern representatives of the kindly and good-natured old-world giants. Seeing this, the malignant ogres, or swart-elves, set to work and attempted in the spirit of keen competition to outrival and excel their betters. The result was a conspicuous failure; and, finding they could do no better by their work, these same demon-giants, in the person of their chief, fell into a wild rage and kicked half-a-dozen holes through the stony heart of their own performance.

It has only to be added that, in the raising or building up of these huge fabrics of rock, the legendary builders, according to the story, had a special object in view. This was to carry a bridge over the waters of the Sound to the shore of the mainland whereby the busy brownies might pass at will from their island quarters and pursue their customary freaks in the vicinity of Hunterston or Southannan Braes. And, strange to say, a corresponding mass of black rock, in the form of a great but much abraded natural dyke, re-appears on the sandy flats of the opposite coast, and bears the name of Black Rock

Leaving behind him these towering walls of rock which have now-a-days-thanks to a well advanced geological science-quite a different and much more truthful tale to tell, the pedestrian or bicyclist readily finds his way northwards, and comes, after another mile of road, to the rocky point of Cleishfarland. This little headland will be easily distinguished by its islet-rock or "cleit' of sandstone, and it seems to have the first part of its name from this very word cleit, meaning a rocky eminence. If this be so, then the full meaning of the whole compound should be "rock-farland," or the foreland distinguished by the presence of a rugged rock. The islet-rock itself is easily seen, for it is easily seen, for it is seldom completely covered by the flood tide. The road now skirts the fine curve of a shingly beach, bounded on the north by a red-sandstone point, outside of which, in the sea, there lies a large black skerry called Black Rock. Ringan's Port is the name of the little creek or haven which lies on the north side of this red-sandstone point, and the place has a special interest on account of its evident proximity to the site of St. Ninian's Chapel. In the near vicinity there is a knoll which has its name from this chapel -KILRANNY,-and there is a distinct tradition which points to a small ancient church in this quarter. Its supposed site presented to view, until recently, certain traces or indications which the former presence of a tiny chapel might explain. Was this the little chapel in which King Hakon heard mass said during the great storm which wrecked so many of his ships in 1264?

BALLOCH BAY

now opens up to view, and also the fine tree-clad eminence of Doun-craig, formerly crowned with a vitrified fort. Portrey farmhouse stands west-three fields off-but it has its name in all likelihood from this fort, -port an raith, the port of the -"rath" or fort. Balloch Pier-erected a few years ago bt the Earl of Glasgow-springs from the rocky point beside the old Ferryhouse harbour, and is only a few yards from the foot of Douncraig. From this point the road runs right north to the Leaddy [leddy] and the famous old-world Cairn which, without a doubt, gives us the name of

TOUMANTENN,

pronounced Tom-an-tenn, and signifying the cairn-grave of the hero. Close by this remarkable cairn the shoreline begins to trend west-north-west for about three hundred yards, and then makes a compass towards the south, and shapes itself into the form of a fine horseshoe bay called White Bay.

The northern extremity of the island has just been passed, and the foot of Glen-aock [áoc] burn has been reached. Here the traveller, if he have mind to do so, may halt and take some rest, for his tour of the island by the great shore-road is already about half accomplished. He may thus at his leisure observe the bright shelly sands of the bay, and the clear streamlet which comes wimpling down the vale. This is the little burn or streamlet named Glen-aock, the waters of which run across the sands of the bay into the sea. It is important to be accurately specific here, for otherwise the stranger might miss the opportunity of inspecting the precise spot where, in the year 1869, a remarkable cluster of

ARCHAIC INTERMENTS

was discovered. The grave-mound or tumulus was of no great height, but it took or had the form of a gently-rising eminence, and it was clad with heather during the first half of the present century. Because of the sandy quality of the soil of the field in which the ancient relics and grave-kists were found, no plough had invaded the sacred deposit, and it was not till a purpose of reclaiming the field was given effect to that an obstacle to the passage of the modern plough led to the most interesting discovery. The "find" consisted of a hero-chief's grave in close association with the graves of two females and that of a youth.

These graves were of the kind called stone-cists by some authors, but kist-vaens by others. Each of them was "formed" of four stone slabs of red-sandstone, with a large overlying slab for a cover, supported by external masonry to relieve the cists. Each cist was floored with a layer of loose, fine white pebbles. The cists were in studied positions; the principal one containing the unburnt bones of a large man, lying nearly north and south, with one on each side tending east and west of similar dimensions, containing respectively an urn and bones reduced by cremation, and from their size and indications probably those of women.

At the foot of the principal cist was a small one containing the bones of a youth and a broken urn, but with no burnt bones, and on the west of that, a cenotaph or empty cist containing a clean urn, but no human remains."

The principal or central cist, containing the teeth, thigh bones, and part of the skull of a tall and stalwart man, was in all probability the last resting-place of one of those old Fomorian sea-rovers who "infested the coasts of Britain during the period of the Roman occupancy, and who, for the most part, were men of Teutonic birth" (Landmarks, page 100). Elatha was the great chief of the Fomorian pirates or sea-rovers who, about the year 50 B.C., swarmed through the German Ocean, and ruled over the Shetland Isles and the Hebrides.

In support of this view must be mentioned the fact that a portion at least of this very field-the shore-field, within the bounds of which the ancient barrow described above was found-bears the name of Nouyorrach, that is, the grave of the pirate or sea-rover. Glen-Aock-an ancient name which belongs to the same locality, and embraces the site of the barrow-can easily be shown to signify the glen of the hero-chief.

It is in reference to this barrow or grave-mound that the following description was given by one of the illustrated weekly journals:-"A cutting was made from east to west, which revealed an undisturbed tumulus of large extent and very peculiar formation. There were three beautifully-formed cists with large overlapping covers, and two smaller ones, each containing articles of interest. the covers of two of the cists were of red-sandstone, carefully and even elegantly rounded into form, and no doubt so worked where quarried, as there were no chippings; while a third was a water-worn slab of large size from the adjoining coast.

The construction of the tumulus, as defined by different coloured soils, placed in uniform positions, and the erection of supports to carry the heavy covers so as to avoid compression of the cists, formed probably unique examples of British-Caledonian construction, and are ante-Roman, or at least of the first or second centuries as to period." -The Graphic, Feb. 26th, 1870.

To find the exact spot on which the barrow stood, let a course be taken right south from the mouth or outlet of the burn,-keeping the burn on the left hand -and the site will be found a short distance south of the centre of the field. The site is nearer to the thorn hedge on the south-only sixty paces from it-than it is to the sandy sea-beach. The cultivated fields in the beautiful vale, as well as the pastures of Aird-hill to the east, are all farmed by the tenant of Portrye- the homestead of which is about half-a-mile to the south of the bay.

Leaving the pleasant shores of White-bay and its archaic associations, the traveller follows the road through the shore meadows, passing successively Wine-bay. Brandy-bay (of smuggling notoriety), Eerie or Ayrie-port, and Skate-bay, gawns-glen burn is crossed a little farther south, and here the "banks and braes" of Figatach come into full view. Bell Bay is opposite the higher and more southern section of these picturesque and copse-clad declivities, which terminate in the lofty terminal rock of Bel-craig-marked by the vestiges of an old stronghold. Less than a quarter of a mile now remains to be traversed in order to reach the magnificent sweep of

FINTRAY BAY.

A pause of a few minutes in this very inviting quarter cannot fail to give delight. If one be a lover of nature, or of solitude, he will find much to interest him as he leisurely moves along this beautiful strand. Numerous species of flowering plants which love the sea air, and an occasional bath in the salt sea-foam, are found all along the upper portion of the beach. Immediately above high-water mark the face of the dunes or sandy links, for over two hundred yards, is firmly bound together by the bent and grasses. Whenever there is a gentle westerly breeze it comes in upon the beach with a freshness that is quite exhilarating. The ceaseless "swash" of the little waves as they curl and break upon the shelly sands, has a music in it that chords and blends harmoniously with the shrill, weird cry of the curlew. Here may be felt the "rapture by the lonely shore," and a sense of all the pleasures which can be found in full communion with nature. Here

Lone Nature feels that she may freely breathe,
And round us and beneath
Are heard her sacred tones: that fitful sweep
Of winds across the steep,
Through wither'd bents-romantic note and clear,
Meet for a hermit's ear,-

The wheeling kite's wild solitary cry,
And, scarcely heard so high,
The dashing waters when the air is still
From many a torrent rill
That winds unseen beneath the shaggy fell,
Track'd by the blue mist well: Such sounds as make deep silence in the heart
For Thought to do her part.-Keble.

The luxury of a bath in the sparkling waters of the bay is often enjoyed by visitors in the morning hours, who may come over from Millport by the short "cut" across the Sheeghans [shee-hans], have their "dip," and return in the brief space of an hour and a-half.

Observe how the upper portion of the beach is clothed with rare and beautiful flowers. Some of the kinds are rare indeed, and two or three of them are of a most captivating beauty. Where id the flower that can rival the delicate hues of the sea-side bell-flower -Convolvulus soldanella- and here it blooms in very considerable abundance? The eryngo or sea-holly springs up from the midst of sand and pebbles, showing a blue, glaucous-tinted foliage that is altogether unique. Silver weeds, which add to their charms by a profusion of bright golden flowers, prank the arid surface of the soil ; sea purslane, coltfoot, and bright scarlet sedums grow in tufts here and there, while the gem of them all-the purple gromwell (Lithospermum maritimum) may occasionally be seen.

Nowhere else could be gathered, a few years ago, such tall and vigorous specimens of the moonwort as those which grew upon the flanks and inner slopes of the dunes. In the marshier piece of background the Osmunda or royal fern reared its stately fronds, but now it is sought for in vain. here, however, the Dutch myrtle, the seggans, and several kinds of salices still hold their own against occasional cullers. So likewise do the strange-looking orchises-called lopper-wintons in the north, -the butterwort, the grass of -Parnassus, and the charming little sundew.

There is a hollow behind the shore-line of dunes or benty hillocks, and from the inland side of this hollow rises a bank clothed with clumps of golden furze interspersed among the heather, while all over the tiny hollows and gentler slopes there springs up a great variety of wild flowers and shrubs indigenous to the island, -the primrose, dog-violet, creeping ivy, small prickly rose, dog-rose, honeysuckle, hawthorn, sloethorn, holly-tree, and rowan-tree.

Pretty shells in amazing variety used to be plentiful on the beach, and are still washed up by the waves in considerable abundance. Razor-bills and unions or clams in almost unlimited quantity used to be taken at the ebb, and formed a welcome addition to the pantry store in many an islander's home.

Aikans in myriad swarmed in the sands here towards low-water mark ; and cockles, garrachans and maryfish swelled the list of what the old folks called "muirach" or shellfish. Most of these sorts may be found still in considerable numbers, but they by no means complete the catalogue of the edible bivalves which these shores supply.

Corallines and many species of lovely sea-weeds may always be gathered here, and many curious marine productions are cast ashore upon the beach, such as the empty egg-cases of the larger buckie, and those strange-looking leathery things called deil's purses.

FINTRAY WELL

is a copious spring or fountain of sweet water, which issues cool and clear from the side of a low-lying ledge of rock near the upper portion of the beach. The spot is about seventy or eighty yards to the north of the "oyce" or foot of the burn which runs down through Fintray-glen and falls into the sea. A famous spring it has been, and still is. It has been known and lauded, and frequented for generations.

The peasants who came this way slaked their thirst at this "fountain in the desert;" lads laden with their basketfulls of "spout-fish" or razor-bills lapped its refreshing waters ere ascending the hill; and numerous parties who; in recent years, have come hither to hold pic-nic beside the bay have charged their kettles with its precious outpourings.

How thankful the traveller often is for a draught of genuine cold water! And here he will find it genuine to the core. The spring is just such an one as that which Ban Macintyre has sung in the following lines:-

"The wild wine of Nature,
Honey-like in its taste,
The genial, fair, thin element
Filtering through the sands,
Which is sweeter than cinnamon,
And is well known to us hunters.
O, that eternal, healing draught,
Which comes from under the earth,
Which contains abundance of God
And costs no money!"

So did George Borrow render the Gaelic verse of the Celtic bard. While we sit by the fountain and take rest for a few minutes, the writer will produce his note-book and read what may, perchance, prove interesting.

"Went on to Fintray-bay. I saw the famous old spring. A flagstone or slab of sandstone has been raised over it-supported on one side by the rock, from between which and the sand bubbles up the spring, and on the other by a flagstone or slab set on edge. The upper side of the covering slab has the inscription-

Doris amara suam non intermisceat undam.
""""""""""" """"""""

The above was written on a beautiful day in April, fourteen years ago. And it is here reproduced, because when the writer was at the spot last summer the inscribed flagstone could not be seen. Possibly the extremely high tide which occurred a few years ago may have swept it clean away and caused it to be lost. The late John Levack, Esq., informed the writer that the inscription itself was cut upon the flagstone by some of the "collegians," and placed by them over the spring. It may be added that a rude stone chair was found here, and might be seen a few years ago within the grounds of Millburn House.

We must now prepare to quit our station by the spring which has interested us so much. But, ere doing so, let us have one glance more at this delectable strand. See how its gleaming sands respond in brightness to the high effulgence of the summer's sun! Bright and shelly is the long beach, glittering with white quartz pebbles and light brown sand. The waves fall upon the beach in ceaseless plash and play, toying with the shells, and making a strangely soft and similar, yet ever-varying, cadence.

"The sea is toying with the shore, his wedded
bride,
And in the fulness of his marriage joy
He decorates her tawny brow with shells,
Retires a space to see how fair she looks,
Then proud, runs up to kiss her."

What a shore for the viking galleys whenever
their owners wished to land! One can almost
fancy he hears the harsh strident grating of their
keels as they plough up the sand and gravel. To
leap ashore and scour the adjacent hills and
dales would be an easy task for the hardy
Norsemen, but not so easy would it be to harry
the homesteads of the brave islands -the
Brandanes of Cumra,-or attempt the forcible
seizure of their lands. If in any chance skirmish
with the natives the sea-rovers had the worst of it,
they would speedly withdraw to their ships, and
prepare for fresh adventures on other coasts.

Should any pedestrian (at this stage of the
journey) desire to leave the circular shore road
and to betake himself homewards by way of
Keillachreasain [keel-a-cressan] and the Shighans,
he should strike a coarse along the southern
verge of Fintray-glen. This will bring him to a well-
built field wall of recent construction, at the first
corner or elbow of which will be seen the
interesting site of Keillachreasain, or the penitent's
cell. Macillhenish [back-ail-hennish], or the field of

the cell of austerity, has been left behind, but it lies along the right bank of the upper portion of the glen, near the spot where a small streamlet joins the glenbrook. Keillachreasain has also, to the west, a little "dyke" or rivulet which falls into the larger stream of Lagalein. Passing southwards along the well-built wall, one finds his way across the lonely pastoral dale of Lagalein,-then, along the eastern side of Clanypott [clanny-paut], or the abott's meadow, and comes, in about twenty minutes from the shore, to the great windy gap which lies between Play Hill and the Shighans [shee-hans]. Millport shore may now be reached from hence in about twelve minutes more.

Those who ride on brake or bicycle must follow the great shore road hence, and on to the Lorne and Millport. On the left hand, as one moves onwards in this direction, rises the "holt" or copse-clad declivity usually called Big-brae; then a great trap dyke is crossed to which the name of Clate-rock attaches itself.

Next, a stretch of similar banks and braes are passed, and also on the right, the pretty creek or inlet of Sheriff's Port, otherwise called Portathro, meaning the port or haven of the chief. Craig-na-feigh, or the crag of the ravens, now towers aloft in full view,- displaying on the left a fine range of precipices; then the "woodbine coach" at the north Douchann is passed, and immediately bald red cliffs begin to appear on the left. Near the south end of these red cliffs there is a little waterfall which, in wet weather, makes a couple of pretty leaps, and may be named the Pishy Mere. About one hundred and eighty yards to the south of this waterfall the vast fragments of a shattered trap dyke will be passed, but most of these were split up for building purposes a few years ago.

The green braes of the Lorne or Kennara Borough now appear on the left, while the rocky shoreline, on the right, shows the skerry or rock-islet (only visible at the ebb) of Allinagreach, or the islet of the "clauba-dows,"-the fine shell-strewn creek called the Shell-hole [better shell-cove],-another little wick or creek named Conch-buckie Bay,-and, lastly, the rocky reefs and ledges of Portahar Point. Bullers-bouies are certain wave-beaten skerries which lie in the sea about midway between the last-named point and the rocky eminence called Knupkurr.

These skerries are clad with fucus and other seaweeds, except, perhaps, their jagged tops, and they have to be carefully avoided by passing wherries. A large schooner named the Fidelity was wrecked on them a few years ago. It may be added that they have their name from an old Danish compound term signifying the billow-inhabiting skerries.

Now we turn the green promontory or headland of the Lorne with its vestiges of old bulwarks, and are immediately on already well known ground. A fine array of handsome villas now occupies much of the old corn-lands of Garbrough, and finds snug quarters under the sheltering brows of the winding copse-clad braes. The Tea-well at the head of Foule-port bight is next passed, and a walk or drive of a very few minutes more brings the traveller back to the point he first started from

(3) FROM THE PIER TO THE GARRISON

Starting, as before, from the Pier, we bend to the right and pass along Stuart-street. Cumbrae Hotel stands on the left, and is really a good house. Visitors to the island may put up here at moderate charges, and find their wants well attended to.

A few paces in advance there is a good Temperance Hotel, and nearby there are two other Hotels. Kelburne Arms is one of these, and being situated a little way up the avenue it has proved to many a sojourner a quiet and happy retreat. This hotel was first started by a Mr. Purves, who acquired the original Free Church of the village, and by a few well devised alterations and additions transformed it into a handsome and commodious Inn. Its appointments are of a superior order, and under the present management the proprietor takes every pains to ensure the comfort of his guests. Millport Hotel is the designation of the other hotel just referred to. It has a good situation on the front line of houses or building, and its windows command an extensive view of the bay and steamboat pier, thus providing a scene of daily interest which not a few take pleasure in studying.

Church-hill road is the next opening on the left, and the handsome church which stands at the head of it is

THE PARISH CHURCH

It was built in the year 1837, and occupies a conspicuous site on the brow of the slope which is called Covans Brae. As the church, at that time, of the whole of the inhabitants of the island-parish (those who attended the Baptist meeting-house excepted), it took the place of the old parish church at Kirktoun,-"Sanct Colmis Kirke."

Bute Terrace is the name of the fine villas or residences which form a line along the brow of Covans Brae, -their gardens and orchards greatly beautifying the sunny slope. Springfield, the second house on the terrace to the east of the parish church, includes within its garden the remarkably fine spring which has always been called Cobbans Well.

In this form of the name of Covan the sound of v has been hardened into that of b, but it is certain that the two forms of the name represent one and the same name. Accuracy is of much importance here, for the next fact to be stated is,- that immediately above the well there was a fine semi-circular slope or brae flanking a dry hill of considerable height, and this same slope or brae-face has, for generations, been called Covans Brae. Now "cavan" or "covan"-Gaelic cabhan, cobhan- signifies a hollow or cavity, a hollow place, a hollow field; yet in some parts of Ulster the word "covan" is understood to mean the very reverse, viz., a round dry hill.

Dr. Joyce, a thorough Celtic scholar and the author of this most reliable work (mentioned in the foot-note), proceeds to explain the origin of this marked difference of usage in regard to the word "covan" or "cavan," and cites some well-known examples of a parallel or similar change. He says-"which of the two meanings it bears in each particular case depends, of course, on the physical conformation of the place." We may, therefore, conclude with some degree of probability that this is the origin of the name of Covan, and that it signifies a dry round hill or hill-brae.

But however likely the above-as to the meaning of the name -may appear, we have to remember that in philology, as in this world generally, things are often not what they seem. Covan, regarded as a name or appellative, may quite plausibly be interpreted "the shrine," or "the reliquary,"-Gaelic comhan [covan].

The patience of the gentle reader who cares little for such investigations is here engaged for a very limited additional space, and we promise not to overtax it by any lengthened philological dichotomy. The question before us has a special interest for some people, and as it is not unlikely that "hereby hangs a tale," it may be as well to attempt a solution of it. Well, be it now said that the name of Covan may be interpreted "the convent cell," "the oratory"-Norse kofin, pronounced kovin.

Bearing this in mind, and looking at the fact of a remarkable discovery, in the near vicinity, of an ancient shrine-grave or solid stone-coffin-with a moderately tall stone cross planted at the head of it - we may not be so very far off the right track if we deem it highly probable that a small chapel or oratory of the Columban age once adorned these shores, and stood at no great distance from the slope of Covans Brae. If any such chapel ever existed, its site may be unknown, and yet "all traces of it" may not be altogether lost. Possibly enough we have in that famous old stone shrine-of saint or abbot-as well as in that peculiarly interesting stone-cross which stood beside it, reliques and "traces" of that substantial kind which none may fail to interpret aright. But besides these-if even these may be claimed-we have in the Cumbraes an old and persistent tradition which points to the locality embraced in the Covans and Trahoun [trah-hoon] as having been the site of an ancient chapel or oratory.

It must be seen by this time that a good deal can be said in favour of the idea of a a "holy place"-be it saint's grave, or chapel, or both-being associated with this locality. -But the half has not been told, and in order to "get up" the other half, or more, let us now take a glance at the name of

TRAH°UN

and the land or lands which it denominates.

On these lands are the two fine villas-Strahoun -Lodge and Cliff Cottage-which occupy a somewhat elevated situation, and constitute the eastern end of Bute-terrace, Near to these villa residences, and on the same lands the beautiful church of the United Presbyterians has recently been erected. It will thus be seen that the lands of Trahoun lie immediately to the west of the Garrison demesne. They extend from the sea-shore on the south, and stretch inland for a considerable distance. It was a nice little property or estate, and was, until a comparatively recent period, held for generations by the Stewarts of Kilwhinlik in Bute.

It now "belongs to the Marquis of Bute, part of it being feued off and included in the village of Millport. It seems to have been the last of the small proprietary holdings in the island, one of the long leases held from old Kilwhinlick having expired not very long ago."

But let it be observed here that it is to the land which extends from the United Presbyterian Church to the sea-shore that the name of Trahoun specially belongs. this includes, of course, the ground on which the eastern part of Guildford-street is built. The sea-beach opposite has been, within recent years, extremely well stripped or cleared of the rough covering which countless stones and boulders had made for it. But at a much earlier time-probably before the close of the last century-a great number of willing hands set to work, and built up out of the rough boulders and loose rocks a capital little pier or jetty for small boats. This small, but very convenient stone pier was called, after the old name of this part of the shore, Trawharry [trah-wharry], and that name it retains to this day. No doubt it has often been mispronounced "Strah-wharry" but just as certainly is it known, and by ample testimony, that the true and genuine old form of this interesting name is

TRAWHARRY.

Promising to return as speedily as may be to this small but useful stone pier, let us now proceed with our study of Trahoun and the old, or even ancient, associations of the place. To this end nothing better occurs to the writer than what he wrote, ten years ago, on this subject. It will be found on page 91 of his Landmarks. A few extracts may be given :-This very interesting name (Trahoun) has been known to me from my earliest years, and I know well how the older natives of Cumbrae pronounce it. The spelling of the name used here is as good as any that can be devised. Drummond, in the new statistical account, writes "Troughewan" for Trahoun. The name is found in several localities throughout the country, and the study of each example, or use of it, helps materially to settle the question of its etymology. Trahoun is in Redesdale, a little way south of the Border; Torheune is in Peeblesshire; and Torquhan is the name of a place in We-dale, or dale of the sanctuary,-a section of the valley of Gala-water. Perthshire supplies another instance of the use of this local name, and three more instances are found in the old Galloway province. Stroquhain is one of the last three referred to, and it shows the name with the letter s corruptly prefixed. Now this same corruption has partly, but only partly, obtained in the instance which our island-study affords. Some people in Cumbrae have been heard to say Strahoun, but the great majority of the older natives of the island always said Trahoun.

Having made a serious study of the Celtic and Norse languages, and having also paid very great attention to the local name now under consideration, the writer has been led to see that "Trahoun" is of Gaelic origin, and that it signifies a penitential station, an oratory or place of prayer, a place of devotion. The name was often applied to the grave-mounds of early Christian teachers and saints. To these grave-hillocks many folk resorted for prayer and penitential devotions

A saint's grave is often called a shrine. In the year 1823 a shrine stone-coffin and cross were found together on the lands of Trahoun. The exact spot where these reliques were discovered is well known to me, and it may be easily found by anyone who will take ten or twelve ordinary paces southwards from the west window of No. 14 Guildford-street, Millport.

We may now say Trahoun Cross and Shrine. But when we do so let us bear in mind that the main idea expressed by the name of Trahoun is that of Tear-hillock-a grave-mound where penitential confessions were made, and where earnest supplications were offered.

It can scarcely be doubted that a church stood near the Tear-hillock or shrine tomb. The amenity and beauty of the locality; the analogy of many chosen sites of ancient churches in Bute, Arran, and Kintyre; the purely ecclesiastical character of the Trahoun shrine-coffin, as Hill Burton and other writers demonstrate; an old and persistent tradition which credits the place or its immediate neighbourhood with the site of an ancient church; recent excavations which have brought to light fragments of bones and an oaken coffin in the vicinity of the western gate of The Garrison,-all these unite in support of the conclusion which ascribes to the lands of Trahoun the site of an ancient church, and associates them with the reliques of a wasted sanctuary.

The devastation of Trahoun may be safely referred to the ninth century or thereabouts. The sacrilege may have been perpetrated by the fierce Vikings, but more likely by the Gallgaels (the offspring of Celtic and Scandinavian alliances), for old chroniclers tell us that these Gallgaels were worse enemies to the churches and their owners than were even the fierce slayers of the North.

As a final suggestion in reference to Covans-brae it may be stated, on the one hand, that those who in ancient times dwelt there and had possession of the underlying fields may have chosen to name their land from the word covan, a shrine-grave, or from the Norse term kofin, a chapel, an oratory; while, on the other hand, those who dwelt a little farther east may have preferred another and a different appellation, viz., Trahoun; and yet both of these two names may have been originally suggested by one and the same object, or closely associated objects, whether it were a chapel, or a saint's grave, or a shrine-tomb within a chapel.

Iona had a Cobhan Cuildich, or Culdee's cell, as these words are interpreted by the writer of the old statistical account of that island. The interpretation is correct, and Dr. Reeves who cites the passage informs us that this building stood upon a reclining plain in a hollow between Dunii and Dunbhuirg, and that its foundations, in the year 1795, measured about sixteen feet by fourteen .-Reeves, Vita Columbae, p 421. The analogy furnished by this instance lends much support to the view which associates our Covansbrae with a very ancient cell or chapel. As a further analogy, let it be noted that the body of Columba of Hy [hee], or Iona, was interred in a "sarcophagus seuarca"-in a shrine-tomb or chest- and that the plundering Northmen, in the year 825, made active search for his "shrine," as it is actually called.

Now this shrine was adorned with precious metals, and had been hid in a dense bush, and underground. When the immediate danger was past the ark or shrine was taken from its place of concealment and soon after removed to Ireland for greater security against the Danes. It was, however, fetched back again; for we have it recorded that, in the year 829, Diarmait, abbot of hy, went to Alba with the minna, or "reliques" of St. Columba.-Ibid., p. 315.

TRAWHARRY PIER

claims our farther attention for a little space. Whoever gives heed to the claim, and acts accordingly, will find his reward in many a pleasant experience. It is well to make this known at an early stage, for otherwise the casual visitor might fail to turn his opportunity to good account.

But now that the hint has been given, he will have himself to blame if he neglects to seeks a closer acquaintanceship with the well-worn stones of this rude but ever-useful stone-jetty. The fine curvature or "line of beauty" which, as to outward form, distinguishes it, the marvellous skill by which so passable a platform of paved work all along its entire length was constructed, the vast labyrinth of dislocated, grotesque and picturesque masses of wave-worn rocks which lie behind it and act as a bulwark or breakwater against the heavy billows and strong south-westerly surge,-these, and other attractive characteristics of the place, soon work for it a way to our hearts, and make it a place of frequent and favourite resort.

When the fishing parties come home at eventide and land on the pier with their well-filled baskets of fish, what a spirit of eager rivalry strikes into the hearts of the spectators, causing not a few of them to decide on the spot that, ere the morrow's sun be high, they too shall be trying their luck on the whiting banks, and striving to draw from the vasty deep, not nameless spirits, but dozens of good haddocks and whitings. When the boat-hiring at our jetty goes on briskly on a fine summer evening, it does one good to sit on one of the big rocks and watch the happy juveniles as they go paddling about blithly in their tiny shallops, or from the same coign of vantage to witness the amusing efforts of some burly citizen from the great commercial city of the West to get himself safely ensconced in the stern-sheets of a bigger row-boat.

Then again, when every pinnace and skiff has cleared out of the quiet haven, and is steering a course for the fishing-ground, or cruising leisurely round the shores and islets, what a pleasure it must be for the solitary occupant of the rock to study the charming features of the marine scenic representation which is pictured before his eyes, and begirt with a framework of cliff and shore as beautiful and rich as such varied lineaments can make it.

The numerous yachts are lying idly at anchor, although every stitch of canvass is set,-their occupants whistling for a breeze, and ready at a moment's notice to slip their moorings and be off like greyhounds of the deep. The swift handsome steamers are never long absent from these shores, and as one of them rounds the point and steams gaily into the bay, what a commotion is made among the shallops and punts by the heavy swell which she leaves in her track.

Here on the left lies a goodly stretch of light-brown sand dotted over with juveniles at play, scattered bevies of young ladies in summer array, and a few casual groups of revered seigniours.

There in front are the grand red cliffs of the Farland glowing with the brightness of an indescribable rosy splendour which flushes every crag, and boss, and brow. It is only for a few seconds as the last level rays of the setting sun fall upon the cliffs, and happy is he who has witnessed some of the finer displays of this superb and fascinating phenomenon. The sea in kames Bay has the sheen of a mirror when the sun at eve strikes upon it and develops the soft gliding movements of a light and almost imperceptible swell, which rolls along in pearly iridescence and breaks upon the strand with a low, sweet, plaintive swish!

Turning his eye more to seaward, the spectator has in full view the magnificent landscape from the Black Rock to Ardneill ; the dark cone of Ailsa Craig in the remote distance, and "doing duty as a watch-tower in the fore-ground;" the grim old castles (once royal residences) of Portincross and Little Cumbrae; the hoary cliffs and terraces of the Little Isle or "lesser" Cumbrae, and the deep green of its slopes and bracken-clad vales.

Farther away to the west, rise the majestic peaks of Arran bathed in a rich warm purple flush of the most enchanting loveliness. "There are the Goatfells to the south, presided over by the patriarch of the group, and himself every inch a

King of Fells. Farther to the right is the beautiful cone of Keenahein or the Hinny's Pap, and right away over its shoulder is the beak-like pinnacle of Ben-oosh. The next peak to right is Sron-a-habar or the Giant's Nose-part of the great A'Chir [ah-keer] or Crested Ridge, and sometimes called Brougham's Nose.

From our station by the pier this polyglot nose will be seen towering high above the col or ridge, which comes between the head waters of Glens Rosa and Sannox. Next in order, turning the eye towards the right, is the towering horn of Keervohr, and showing, even from our present point of view, somewhat of the trident-like appearance which the view from the four granite boulders on the Lamlash road betrays. Right beneath Keervohr lies a vast under-world of shadow, filling almost throughout the great hulk-like trough of Glen Sannox, and reaching far up into the dark recesses of Cornawhee.

The next to hand, on the right, ate the four sharp and lofty pikes of Caym-na-calyie or The Witch's Stride, and which are feigned in common story to be the facial features of the "Giant asleep."

Following up this fancy the popular eye has traced the outline of the giant's breast in the next great elevation to the right, and while some place a buckler with bosses on the breast of the giant, for his protection in sleep and long siesta, others feign that his massive hands are clasped in prayer, and that these resting on his well expanded chest form the huge knuckle-like projections which culminate in the peak of Greenan Ahval." -Landmarks, p. 195.

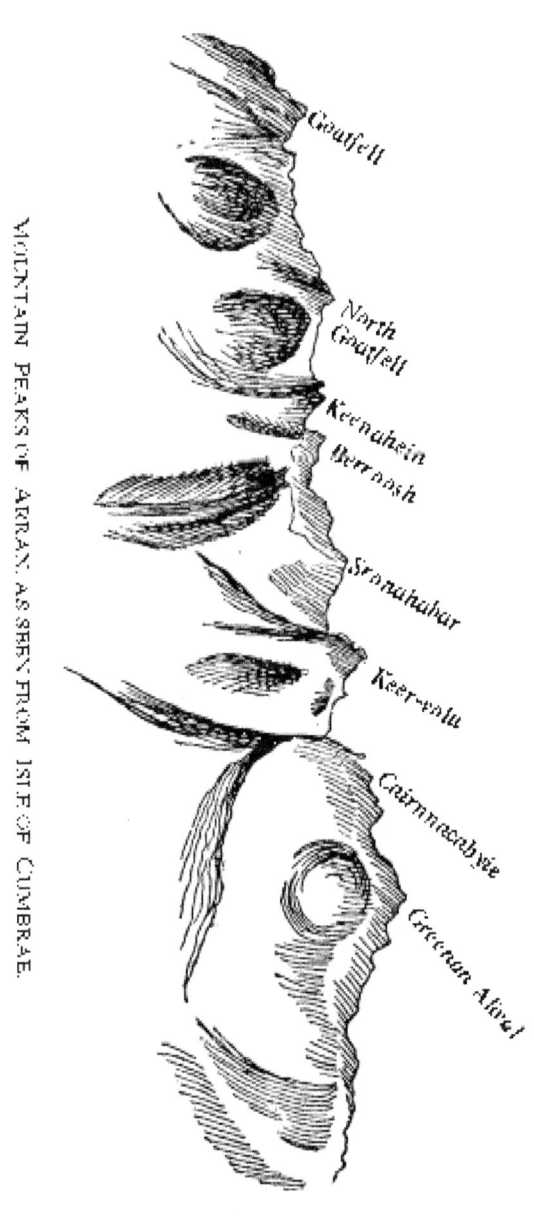

MOUNTAIN PEAKS OF ARRAN, AS SEEN FROM ISLE OF CUMBRAE.

Goatfell

North Goatfell

Keenahein

Berroosh

Sronahabar

Keer-valu

Cairnnacabyie

Greenan Ahiel

Here is a recently-made sketch of the striking

52

view last presented, but it differs from it by being taken in the morning. It may enable ant interested party to make out more distinctly than in the evening some of the peaks and ridges of the Arran Fells. -Morning, 9 o'clock: A few minutes ago there was a good deal of mist on the mountain, but it is now seen rising fast upwards into the deep blue. The great corrie lying in the bosom of the mountain between light-coloured ribs and scars. Above the corrie, and to the right of it,

Keenahein shows beautifully distinct against the white fleeces of floating mist, and similarly Suy Fergas displays its handsome peak against the white background of curling mist, which fills the Scallop-shell corrie near the summit ridges of Greenan Ahval.

Scenes such as these cannot be contemplated, or even simply beheld, without leaving a refreshing and exhilarating effect upon heart and mind. the cheering influence of sunshine and the fresh sea-air laden with ozone comes, too, in aid of these happy experiences, and the visitor who has once made a familiar acquaintance of Trawharry and its grotesquely fashioned rocks will be sure to repair often to the spot and refresh (if need be) the jaded energies of mind and body.

He may also, thereby, lay up in store for future remembrances or contemplation a rich fund or treasure of bright and pleasing reminiscences, which shall be to him a solace and delight when the claims of business or of duty carry him far hence. It was under such circumstances that the writer-long familiar with the scenes he has here attempted to depict, and at one period long removed from them-sought to improve the occasion of a fresh but only too brief visit by penning the following verses:

CUMBRAE REVISITED.

On a day of mellowed brightness,
In September's golden prime,
Scenes of beauty so impressed me
As to weave themselves in rhyme.

'Twas at grey Trawharry's station
Scenes familiar spread to view.-
Rocks and sands and headlands hoary,
Radiant each with many a hue.

Oft have I in dales so distant
Seen, as in a summer season,
Pictured clear upon the mirror
Of my soul's delighted vision,

Cumbrae's bosky braes and woodlands,
Bending round its shelly shores,
Girdling all as with a setting
Framed of valleys green and torrs.

And the picture gemmed with islets,
Yachts and boats and steamers too,
Fishers casting nets, and children
Plunging in the brine so blue.

But the vision soon was driven
From the page of Fancy's book
By the toil and cares of manhood,
Ever claiming glance or look.

So I joy once more to gaze on
Solid rocks and yellow sands,-
All the grand mosaic fashioned
By the great Creator's hands.

All the myriad glancing facets
Shimmering on the eye of ocean,
And reflecting in its clearness
Heaven's blue, or clouds in motion.

As familiar friends each feature
Seems to smile a welcome true;
And a still small voice repeateth
Legends of the old and new.

Let me sit, and look, and listen
While my Maker speaks to me
Living truths from rocks and greenwoods,
Or the voices of the sea.

There is often more in a name than some
people imagine, and when a name which has
become familiar to us is easily pronounced or has
a euphonious ring about it, it is all the more likely
to become the centre or nucleus of inspiring
associations. It may therefore be well to point out
the correct pronunciation of the name of
Trawharry, and to declare against a corruption of
it which locally obtains. Trawharry is properly
pronounced when the first syllable tra (not traw) is
so sounded as to rhyme with the first
monosyllable in the lyrical refrain,-"Tra la la." The
remaining portion of the name [wharry] has a very
short sound given to the vowel a, as in the final
syllable of "organ," where the a is sounded very
like the short u in "gun."

As it is possible enough that the name of
Tra-wharry [tra-wharry] is simply a Lowland-Scots
form of the Gaelic traigh gharbh, meaning the
rough shore, or the rough strand; and further, as
it is expedient that a settled orthography of this
local name should prevail, all who are friendly to
the doing of things decently and in order, are
invited to follow and adopt the old orthographic

form-Trawharry. In connection with particular point or question it has only to be added that "Strawharry" is the corrupt form of the name, as referred to above. It is a corruption, certainly, that one has to be on his guard against, yet it must be acknowledged that the corruption has got a footing so firm as to give only a moderate hope of its being eliminated for years to come.

THE GARRISON.

As the visitor leaves the sea-shore and approaches the head of the little pier which has proved so interesting, he will observe in front, and towards the right, a large elegant mansion or edifice. This is The Garrison. It is the residence of the Earl of Glasgow, one of the two noble proprietors of the island. As one of the seats or residence of Lord Glasgow-a descendant of one of the old barons of Cumbrae-this charming sea-side residence cannot fail to elicit interest and admiration.

The view of it which is obtained from the picturesque rocks of Trawharry is considered one of the finest. The rich architectural features and fine proportions of the building are here seen to the best advantage ; while the general effect is greatly enhanced by a dark-green background of trees, which gives tone and character to the picture. On the rising ground, to the right of the view, a noble pile of exquisitely beautiful buildings arrests the eye and engages the high admiration of the beholder. This is The Collegiate Church and College, founded in 1849 by the Hon. George Frederick Boyle, who became in 1869 Sixth Earl of Glasgow.

Another fine view of The Garrison may be had from the north-west angle of the Beautiful demesne within the bounds of which stands the earl's residence. To reach the spot whence this particular view is obtained, let the visitor pass up the avenue which runs along the western side of the Garrison grounds, and take his station on the braeface or slope adjacent to the Public-school. Taking advantage of this somewhat elevated station in order to make a few observations on the pleasant vale which lies between our present standpoint and the Cathedral Church, the first thing which falls to be noticed is the wide and charming prospect which the situation commands.

On the right hand many yachts and smaller craft at anchor, in front the Garrison-much enlarged and beautiful within recent years-the dagger-like point of the Farland with its lofty red crags and precipices, the long wooded steep of Innean-brae, and-more to the left-the farmhouse of Breaghogh near the head of the Garrison vale, the fine green hill of Gouards farther off, and the higher eminences of Tarraigh and Play Hill. A glimpse of

St. Andrew's Church embowered among trees may be caught, and it is interesting to know that in the vicinity of this chapel there was found a small flake or slab of stone with an incised cross upon it. The fact recals us to the consideration of the ancient conditions of the vale immediately before us, and it was this which the writer had in view when calling upon the visitor's attention for a moment to this beautiful valley of Breaghogh. Did the "grey forefathers" who dwelt here in distant epochs have any special fancy for so fertile a dale? Did the beauty and amenity of the valley and its shell-sprinkled sea-strand have any charms for them? Did they plant their bee-hive cottages on the green machar or plain where it bordered with the sea, or did they prefer the shelter of the cliffs and bushy declivities of Trahoun?

These are questions for which no direct answer can be found, but the rude archaic pillar-stones of the Breakough and the numerous grave-kists under the great Cairn of Marlfield unite to tell us that men and women of the remote past chose one of the fairest dales in the island for a dwelling-place, and assigned two of its sunniest nooks to the dust that was dear to them.

The flora of the shore-head along Garrison-bay was, until recently, about as full and varied as that of Fintray-bay. The vast amount of sand carried off during the last fifty years from this beach (for good and useful purposes, no doubt) has allowed the sea to encroach upon the land and sweep away the pretty sea-pinks, sea-daisies, and other shore-loving flowers, the grace and beauty of which lent an additional attraction to a quiet stroll along "these yellow sands." But one source of interest and pleasure, which it is not easy for man to touch with injurious effect, may be found here when the tide has ebbed to its farthest limit.

The sea-weeds, sea-anemones and other marine productions are as plentiful and as beautiful as ever. In the shoal water inside of the Allens there is a never-failing "harvest of the sea," in the gathering of which not a few take delight. Low water is the time to secure the prettiest "objects of the sea-shore," but sometimes a storm comes to the help of the collector, and pours at his feet the purple shells and the more empurpled plumes of ocean.

As to the edible shell-fish, comparatively few are now to be found, and these are almost entirely confined to the Rigg, a long low sandy ridge clad with the green "zostera," which appears above water at the very lowest ebbs, and over which one may walk dry-shod to the nearest of the two Allens.

Returning to the Garrison, a few notes as to its history may now be given. It seems to have been built nearly a century ago. The Old Statistical Account of the island and parish was written in the month of May, 1793, but although the writer of that account speaks of the anchorage at the Allens as "the rendezvous of the Royal George revenue cutter-Captain James Crawford," he does not once mention the name of Garrison.

This, however does not make it quite certain that the original house of this name did not exist in the year mentioned. A good authority (Jamieson) states that the great cairn of Marlfield was removed prior to 1807, and as it appears that the stones of this cairn were used in the building of The Garrison, the inference is clear that the mansion was built before the year 1807. But whatever the date of its erection, it is certain that the original house of this name was built on its present site by the Captain James Crawford mentioned above.

The gallant captain had a lease of the ground from Lord Bute, in token of which he was bound to present a white rose (if required of him) to the superior, on the eleventh of July of each year.

In the year 1819 The Garrison was purchased by the Fourth Earl of Glasgow, who "made very extensive additions," and otherwise greatly improved it. Coming down to more recent times, it may now be mentioned that the present Earl "has bought up the interest of the heirs of Captain James Crawford." Eaton Reid, writing twenty-two years ago, says: "'The rise of the town (of Millport) was mainly due to the bay having become a station for the Revenue Cutter, the first of which was a two-masted boat and was called the Cumbray wherry, commanded by Captain Andrew Crawford.

His son, James Crawford, afterwards assumed the charge of the station, and commanded the Royal George cutter. He obtained a piece of ground from the Marquis of Bute on a lease destined to subsist during the lifetime of the lessee, and of his brother and sisters, brothers-in-law, or any child of either of them, for payment of a rose on the 11th july annually. The captain built thereon a house with a wall in front, having gun-ports furnished with cannon, and called his place "The Garrison," a name which it still retains." -
Hist. Co. Bute, p.83.

Within the last decade the present Earl of Glasgow has greatly enlarged and beautiful this distinguished-looking residence. He has also erected two main entrance Gateways of very handsome design and solid construction. Their architectural features are indeed superb, and command the admiration of every one. The Effect of the crenelated device in giving beauty and lightness to these massive structures is very

63

marked, and one cannot look upon them without feeling the pleasure which only perfect art can give. Over each archway an exquisite piece of sculpture represents the noble Earl's Coat of Arms-an eagle displayed, with two heads, for Boyle, and the motto Dominus providebit. A handsome porter's lodge has been built beside the western gateway ; commodious stables have been constructed on the rising ground more to the north, many other improvements have been made, and, lastly, a strong retaining wall has been built round the whole demesne.

(4) THE CATHEDRAL CHURCH AND COLLEGE.

Forty years ago as the villager turned up the "green loaning," which ran along the eastern verge of the Garrison bounds, he came in a few seconds to a fine open space, where was a Green of ample dimensions. It had a fine fountain of clearest spring water, and was well sheltered from the rough winds by the wooded eminence on the east, and by the tall saughs or willow-trees which lined the brook on the west.

This little brook came wimpling down the vale, now on one side of the loaning, now on the other. Just where it approached the well, and near the north-west corner of the green there was quite a little swamp or quagmire-something more than a mere wal e'e-but green withal, and abounding in floating patches of the loveliest green duckweed and watercress. -The beautiful iris or seggan found here a congenial habitat, and little clumps of the basket-maker's willow overhung the clear rivulet, and waved their long lancet-shaped leaves in the summer gale.

See the soft green willow springing
Where the waters gently pass,
Every way her free arms flinging
'O'er the moist and reedy grass.
Long ere winter blasts are fled,
See her tipp'd with vernal red,
And her kindly flower display'd
Ere her leaf can cat a shade.-Keble.

But in attending to some of its accessories, the Green itself must not be forgotten. It had a beauty all its own. Green as only turf in the Western Isles can be, starred and gemmed all over with a rich profusion of buttercups and daisies,-"with cowslips and with daisies pied"-it had besides, in early springtime, a glory of golden furze or whin bloom, which few who have beheld it can ever forget.

It was the delight of schoolboys to roam unchecked through this little bit of wilderness, explore every whin-bush in search of linnets' nests, or gather in their season the shining, ebony berries which they called black-boyds. A narrow cart-track passed diagonally across this veritable People's Park, and led over the rising ground to the south of the College. Skirting the sunny side of the hill of Torr-mor (on the breast of which stands the Cathedral), it passed a-down the gentle slope, crossed the Leny-burn, and held straight over the meadows to

THE MAIDEN KNOWE.

On the north side of the Green which has just been described, there rose a gently ascending field with a beautiful sunny exposure, the "rigs" of which were clothed every summer with corn in the ear and with that prolific esculent which is as the "staff of life" to many a peasant's family.

Often indeed, in early life, has the writer of these pages spent hours at a time "on duty" here, and on such occasions many a noxious weed or plant of baleful hue suffered for it. It was but a premonition of the time-then near at hand-when the spiritual husbandman, or keeper of the vineyard, should do his part (and within the walls of the sacred building about to be erected on the spot) in the faithful preaching of the gospel, and in the uprooting of those pernicious weeds and roots of bitterness which alas ! are the bane of many a heart.

Thou Spirit, who the Church didst lend
Her eagle wings, to shelter in the wild,
We pray Thee, ere the Judge descend,
With flames like these, all bright and undefil'd,
Her watchfires light,
To guide aright
Our weary souls, by earth beguil'd.

So glorious let Thy Pastors shine,
That by their speaking lives the world may learn
First filial duty, then divine,
That sons to parents, all to Thee may turn,
And ready prove
In fires of love,
At sight of Thee, for aye to burn. - The Christian
Year, St. John Baptist's Day.

And, as already hinted, that time arrived right
soon. It was in the early summer of 1849 that the
first sod was cut, and a few weeks more saw the
deep-seated foundations of the Cathedral Church
of the Holy Spirit laid. Vast and ponderous were
the blocks of stone which formed the solid
substructure of the tall and graceful spire. In due
season the walls both of church and college
began to appear above ground,and the noble
founder had the satisfaction of seeing the good
work carried out on its happy completion.

Desiring with all his heart to do justice to the
description of this "holy and beautiful house," as

well as to the associated Institution or College, the writer deems he cannot serve his purpose better than by making two or three quotations which have special reference to the subject on hand. And the first of these shall be from the pen of the late John Eaton Reid, Esq., a gentleman whose memory is held in much honour by the people of Cumbrae.

Writing in the year 1864 this accomplished author says :- "The most prominent, however, of the ecclesiastical buildings in Cumbrae are those founded by the Honourable G. F. Boyle (now Earl), consisting of the church and college, together with the schools adjacent, and the little church of St. Andrew's within the policies, all in connection with the Episcopal Church of Scotland, and under the direction of the Bishop of Argyle and the Isles, who is Provost of the College. Episcopal worship first took place in St. Andrew's Chapel on 1st August 1848, and on Whit-Tuesday, 1849, the first stone of the College Church was laid.

The Buildings, which are an honour to the architect, W. Butterfield Esq., London, present a very imposing appearance, situated as they are in grounds laid off with much taste. The church occupies the centre, and is of most beautiful and chaste design, surmounted by a tower and spire of very elegant proportions, 123 feet in height, containing three fine-toned bells and a clock of excellent workmanship. The nave of the church is plain, and evidently intended so as that aisles may be added should circumstances require it. Between the nave and the chancel is a most beautiful stone screen having brass gates and granite pillars supporting the tracery and embossed cross, while the chancel and organ aisle are highly decorated and ornamented with stained-glass windows, producing a fine effect ; the roof also is painted to represent the ferns and flowers abounding on the island. The southern wing of the building is called the Canons' House, and is occupied by the clergy and students ; it contains also the library and reading-rooms, while the northern division is occupied by the Vice-provost as a collegiate residence.

The college buildings were taken possession of by the students and choristers upon the 18th November 1850 , and on Whitsunday, 1851, the church was first opened for worship. Much praise is due to the Hon. Mr. Boyle, for the great exertions which he made during the infancy of this church, with which his name as founder will be inseparably connected, and the Dowager-Countess of Glasgow has also shown throughout a warm and liberal interest in the prosperity of the institution. Mr Boyle is now, however, ably supported by the clergy of the college, namely, the Right Rev. Bishop Ewing, Provost, the Rev. J. G. Cazenove, Vice-Provost, the Rev. J. P. Keigwin and others, including the Rev. H. H. Richardson, chaplain to the Dowager-Countess of Glasgow, and Mr James T. Vidgen, the organist and conductor of the music.-Hist. Co. Bute, p. 157.

Hugh Macdonald writing in the year 1857-seven years before Reid-speaks first of the "magnificence" of this group of buildings, and of the "admiration" which their architectural beauty excites. Then he goes on to say :-"With that enlightened curiosity to which our readers are so much indebted, we resolved, if possible, to have a peep for ourselves at the sacred structure. Accordingly when the matin chimes are inviting the faithful to prayers (which they do every morning), we repair to the chapel of the College.

The grounds are extensive and beautifully laid out in lawns, terraces, and parterres, which are adorned with the choicest shrubs and flowers. Everywhere there are evidences of the most correct taste. The walks are neatly trimmed, the lawns as carefully shaven as the beard of an exquisite, while the borders are perfect models of floricultural skill.

On a gentle elevation over-looking the town and the bay, and commanding a noble prospect beyond, are the collegiate buildings. They are of the purest Gothic : every characteristic feature being as strictly embodied in the design as if the salvation of the artist depended on the perfection of his work. Everything is on a small scale, however, and the effect upon our mind is rather the delight which a pretty model might produce, than the solemnising influences which do hedge about the grand old piles of other years. But the bell has ceased, and we must enter the sacred edifice.

Within, there is a perfect picture in miniature of the mediæval chapel. We have the stained glass windows 'casting a dim religious light,' the tesselated floor, the naked oaken beams above, the alter with all the prescribed accessories, crucifixes of gold, and of stone, of various fashions, with we know not what all besides. It is, in fact, quite a little gem of a chapel. . . . After walking round the structure again and again, admiring its fair proportions, particularly those of the spire, which is a perfect study of elegance, we take our leave of the hallowed grounds, and return once more to the everyday world."-Days at the Coast, p. 223.

Dr. J. G. Cazenove, who did a great and good work in this church and college for many years, writing in 1872, says : -"The objects of the foundation [of this church and college] are stated by the founder, in the preamble to the statues, to be the worship of the Most High GOD, the due administration of the Sacraments of His Church, and the preaching of His Holy Word in a temple reared to His honour and glory ; together with the maintenance or education of clergy, or those who may be looking forward to the holy work of CHRIST'S ministry, whereby the spiritual necessities of the country may be relieved, the sacrifice of praise offered to GOD, and the unsearchable riches of CHRIST be made known.

The Isle of Cumbrae is situated in the Firth of Clyde, nearly opposite Largs. the views from Cumbrae, more especially that of Arran, are eminently grand. The population of the island is about 1,600, though this number is more than trebled during the season. Communication with the mainland is chiefly carried on by means of the steamers to Wemyss Bay.

The college at Cumbrae forms a conspicuous object in approaching the island ; and as it is visited by hundreds, during the summer months more especially, the following brief account of the Institution and its buildings-and more particularly of its most attractive feature, the CHURCH-will probably be acceptable.

Landing at the pier, and proceeding along the shore, the visitor passes on the left the Garrison, the residence of the Earl of Glasgow, the founder of the college. A road on the left, passing between the grounds of the Garrison and those of the College, leads to the principal gate of the later, at which notices are affixed of the hours of service in the church, and also of the time at which strangers are admitted to see the place - viz., from 1 to 3 p.m.; but admission may be obtained at other times on special application.

Passing through the gate, the visitor finds himself within an enclosure of about twelve acres, and directly in front of the Collegiate Church and buildings, placed at the top of a succession of terraces, approached by flights of steps.

The thickly-wooded and irregular copse, seen on the right from the entrance-gate, will give an idea of the nature of the ground originally. Towards the left is seen, standing prominently out, the Cemetery, the ground of which is entirely of artificial construction. The solid gate-way at its entrance is called the "Lich-Gate," a name signifying, in Saxon, the porch under which the corpse is rested while preparations are made for the interment.

From this point, too (for we suppose the visitor to be still pausing at the entrance-gate of the grounds), the nest view of the entire group of the college buildings is obtained. The church occupies the centre, stretching from east to west, as was the ancient rule ; the west window is seen facing the spectator. The southern wing of the building is called the Canon's House, as being the residence of the clergy, who are members of the college. Here also are lodged any other clergy residing for the purpose of retirement and study, or as guests, as also the Theological Students,- that is, candidates for Holy Orders, who, after having been educated at the University, are pursuing here the studies necessary for their sacred calling.

The plateglass windows, seen in the lower part of the building, give light to two spacious libraries, allotted to the clergy and the students respectively. The dormer windows in the roof light their bed-rooms and studies, ranged on either side of a corridor running the entire length of the building. In the bell-turret, which with good architectural effect, breaks this length, are the bells, which are rung at certain hours for rising and retiring, for the private prayers of the college, &c. Below are the kitchen and other offices, and a hot water apparatus for heating the church and the college in winter.

Both church and college are built of the delicately coloured freestone of the Island, procured from a quarry within the grounds, the property of the Earl of Glasgow. The northern wing of the buildings is occupied by young men, either members of, or preparing to enter the English Universities ; its arrangement is similar to that of the south wing.

On going up the flights of steps at the end of the broad entrance walk, and passing round the east side of the college, a cloister is seen forming two sides of a small quadrangle, intended to be completed hereafter, while beside it appear the end of the College Hall, and that of the Chapter House adjoining the church, having five lancet windows.

The Church is entered at the south-western door, under a well-proportioned tower and spire, 123 feet in height, containing three bells.

There are in the interior of every church two parts at least : the larger or western part, called the Nave, occupied by the people ; and the eastern, called the Chancel or Choir, occupied by the clergy and others engaged in conducting the service, partly by the Alter, or Holy Table, at which the Holy Communion is celebrated. The easternmost part of the choir, where the altar stands, is called the Sanctuary.

The nave of the church has plain chairs for the use of the people ; it is lighted by four windows on the south side, and one at the west, filled with stained glass, the gift of those who had been employed in building the church and college. There is a row of several hundred glass-lights running round the nave. The pulpit stands on the north side ; sermons are preached twice or three times a day on Sundays and Festivals, in this church or at St. Andrew's. The nave is separated from the choir by a stone screen, or partition, having brass gates. The pillars on either side of the gates are of polished Aberdeen granite, and branch out above into tracery of stone, having in the middle an embossed cross.

The Choir, and especially the Sanctuary, as being the place where the highest ordinance of the Christian religion takes place, is ornamented more richly than the Nave. We are privileged under the Christian dispensation to offer the best and most beautiful works of man's head and hands to GOD in His Sanctuary.

The Alter, or Holy Table, accordingly, is adorned with rich and appropriate vestments, varying according to the season or festival ; and the vessels used in the celebration of Holy Communion, and the Cross placed upon the Alter, are of precious metals, studded with jewels.

The candles standing on it signify the CHRIST is the true Light of the world. The small stone table, on the north side, called the Credence-table, is for the bread and wine before they are consecrated. The walls of the Choir are inlaid, partly with a white material resembling porcelain, partly with encaustic tiles, of delicate tints of green, red, &c.,

disposed diamond-wise, in horizontal lines. The floor has various patterns of encaustic tiles. On the roof, are represented the ferns and flowers abounding on the Island.

The windows in the choir are all of stained glass. The east window contains representations of the four Evangelists, and of St. Columba and St. Augustine. The two south windows were preserved as memorials. the window nearest the Nave represents the Crucifixion of our LORD, with the words, "It is finished." The next, of which the colouring is peculiarly rich, represents our LORD'S Resurrection. On the north side is the organ, behind a screen of wrought iron. The choir is lighted, when necessary, by gas-lights, placed round the Choir-arch, and by a Corona, or Chandelier, in the centre.

To the right and left of the choir are vestries, or sacristies, containing the vestments for the Clergy, and other things for the celebration of the services of the church.

The service in the Collegiate Church [the cathedral] is choral. The ritual is modest. In the year 1854, the Bishop of the Diocese, Dr. Ewing, kindly consented to a set of regulations, according to which these services were to be conducted. these regulations have been strictly adhered to. Consequently the services have remained for eighteen years in precisely the same condition : a circumstance which in these days of change is probably very rare. The Scottish Liturgy is used at the Communion Service excepting on the first Sunday in the month, when the English rite is employed at the Mid-day celebration, either at the Collegiate Church, or at that of St. Andrew's, the smaller place of worship, which is used for parochial offices, and considered as the parish Church of Episcopalian residents in the Island, who do not live within the college."

The stated or regular services in this church have been much appreciated, during the last three decades, by residents on the island as well as by numerous visitors from the mainland. Grateful, indeed, have many Presbyterian auditors and worshippers been, not only for "the blessings of so elevating a form of worship, but likewise for sermons heard there, which have, for the most part, been uncontroversial, and practical in their tendency."

Not a few learned men have pursued their studies with much success within the walls of the institution, and the continuous cultivation of sound learning has certainly not been neglected. Here the rev. Philip Freeman (now the Ven. the Archdeacon of Exeter) wrote the first part of his "Principles of Divine Service," and here also Provost Cazenove added his "Mohammedanism" and several other valuable works to the higher literature of the age. A large proportion of the alumni of the college have distinguished themselves, and "have likewise received much encomium at English ordinations. It has received at moderate rates, numerous clergymen needing rest and change. Such inmates have, in almost every instance, either returned, or have recommended some other friends to follow their example. many of these visitors, including some of the honorary canons, have been men of much eminence for learning and influence. We may name especially the late Bishop Low, the Revs. John Keble and Thomas Bowdler."-Provost Cazenove.

The scenery on every side of the church is of the most charming description. The views of Arran to be obtained from its precincts are as impressive as they are sublime. Torr-mor is the old name of the hill, upon the southern shoulder of which stands the sacred edifice. The Tarraighs are the two hills right north. Play-Hill is more to the north-west ; and to the left of the great gap the green mounts, called Shighans or Fairy-Mounts, extend themselves.

Fauld Makneansh lies in front of the Play-Hill, and comes close down to the homestead of Braighogh farm. Its name has a special interest, as it certainly signifies the field of the festival or play.

Taken along with the name of the adjacent Play-Hill, it points to the games and sports which the people were wont to engage in on festival days. Feilcolm Knowe, or the knoll of the festival of St. Columba, is on the lands of Kirktoun, about half-a-mile to the south-west.

Standing between the north-west angle of the cathedral and the magnificent Celtic cross which faces the lych-gate, one obtains a fine view of the Garrison and its picturesque grounds, the housetops of a portion of the town, the school and schoolhouse, the churches on the terrace, the Braes o' Lorne, the bay and its islets, the hoary cliffs and verdant uplands of Little Cumbrae, and, in the distance, the majestic peaks of Arran. The whole picture is one of pleasing and almost unequalled beauty, and its more striking features cannot fail to grave themselves deeply on the memory.

As a fitting sequel to what has been already said it may now be stated that the Collegiate Church of Cumbrae was consecrated as the Cathedral of the Isles on the third day of May, 1876, and is now also recognised as the pro-Cathedral of Argyll.

TRAHOUN CROSS.

The upper portion of this very ancient and most interesting stone-cross may be seen in the cemetery of the cathedral. It is a genuine relic, authenticated beyond dispute. It has been cut or hewn, when entire, out of a large slab of white sandstone similar to that of the adjacent sea-shore.

The portion of the shaft of the cross which is here preserved is 17½½ inches in length, while the length of the cross-bar is 19 inches. The width of the shaft below the arms is nine inches. In design it is plain, without interlacing knotwork or other ornament except a single incised line or groove running along near to the outer edge or verge. Originally, and when entire, this cross was (of a certainty) about five feet in length, the remaining or absent portion of its shaft is lost.

In the year 1823, as described above, p.39, the entire cross was found standing in the earth Close to the head of a very large shrine stone-coffin on the lands of Trahoun. Some labourers, seeking stone for building purposes, were removing a thick covering of sand which strong easterly winds had blown from the neighbouring strand into a vast heap or mound, and when these workmen had penetrated to "a depth of five or six feet" they came upon the cross and the

<=" p="">

associated stone-coffin. The cross was taken up from its erect position at the head of the Coffin, and laid upon the sand-heap, where by some mischance it was accidentally broken. The lost portion of the shaft, it cannot be doubted, met the same fate as the stone-coffin, both being used for building materials. Both, however, may yet be recovered. If ever the day comes when a certain couple of houses in the village shall be pulled down, with a view to their re-erection, then will be the opportunity to search for the lost treasures. Drummond, writing in the year 1840, says that the upper portion of this cross was at the time in his possession (N. S. A., Vol. v.)

Three years afterwards he left the Manse, and his successor-Rev. Alexander Marshall found the sacred fragment on the manse premises. It was carefully preserved by this latter incumbent of the parish church, and before his decease in 1866 the precious relic was passed over as a gift into the hands of the Earl of Glasgow. Its genuineness is undoubted. The late Mr. George Paterson, who was one of the workmen present at the first discovery of the cross, knew it well, and he personally testified to the writer that this identical fragment of a stone-crosses, in very truth, the upper portion of Trahoun Cross.

THE SHRINE-COFFIN.

As a sequel to the above details regarding the ancient cross, a brief description shall now be given of the shrine stone-coffin with which it was so closely associated. This latter was upwards of eight feet in length, by two-and-a-half feet in breadth, and eighteen inches in thickness (or depth). It was, of course-as being manifestly a solid stone coffin or sarcophagus- hollowed out by the chisel of the stone-hewer, and the exact spot for the head was formed, or scooped out, into a beautiful cavity. Inside there was, at the waist, a slight ridge running across the bottom, dividing the whole length into two unequal parts, the one three, and the other five feet. The intelligent informant, who was present at the discovery of this stone-coffin, said that it would hold a man of six feet, and that it reddish soil beneath it.

The stone lid or covering of the coffin was nowhere to be seen, and it is certain that at some period in the remote past its own proper stone lid had been removed. Close by the wider or head-end of the shrine-coffin there stood the cross described above-"its ornamental side facing it, its foot sunk about two feet into the earth, and its head rising above the stone about one-and-a-half feet."

Drummond, who wrote the words just quoted, also goes on to say that "the larger Stone (the shrine-coffin) was it immediately broken into pieces of more convenient size for purposes of building;" and another informant or witness (Geo. Paterson) states that these very pieces or fragments must have been used in the construction of the two houses which Gilbert Lennox built.

It is scarcely possible to turn away from so captivating a theme without first hazarding some remarks on the probable circumstances which led to the desolation of Trahoun shore, and to the unhallowed rifling of what must have been the tomb of some eminent "coarb" or Cumbrae ecclesiastic. If the missing stone-lid of our shrine-coffin were (as is extremely probable) anything like the exquisitely carved cover of the famous Govan one, it may indeed have seemed, in the eyes of some Norse reivers, worth carrying off but whether it were snatched away by ruthless marauders, or removed as a precious memento by pious hands to such a place as St. Bees, it seems now only too certain that it is irretrievably lost. It is remarkable, and not a little significant, that the ancient cross was found entire, and not only entire, but well planted in the ground as a "head-stone" cross.

One naturally infers from the above narrative that violent hands had sacrilegiously disturbed the quiet of the grave, scattered the sacred deposit, and dragged the great, heavy, enshrining stone to some little distance from its original position. Who then planted or replanted the cross on the very spot in which it was found sixty-three years ago? Who was the worthy, venerable churchman for whom so honourable-nay, so distinguished an interment had been devised and executed more than a thousand years ago ?

Questions like these are not easily answered, but even if some little ray of light can be thrown upon them, the focussing of the irradiating beams would far out-run the limits of these pages. It may be well, however, at this stage, to recall to mind the fact that there is an old, distinct, and persistent tradition which attaches an ancient church or religious house to the shore lands of Trahoun, and does so with sufficient definiteness to warrant one in fixing its site at no great distance from that of these relics.

Did the tradition stand alone it might be held or accounted a matter of small moment, but backed as it is by the discovery of such significant relics it asserts its claim to be heard. Well, and what if we listen to its voice? Why this-that somewhere about fifteen centuries ago, and on a certain day, a tiny bark is seen crossing the "silver streak," which separates Cumbrae from the mainland, and making straight for its island shore.

The attention of the natives is arrested, they crowd the beach, and soon witnessed the landing of a young and active herald of the cross. Escorted by a motley group, the new-comer makes his way to the dwelling of the Chief, and tells him of the glad tidings he is commissioned to bear to him. Then he craves a boon of the lord of the island-begs a little plot of ground on which he may build a habitation for himself, and a house of prayer to which all may come. This, or something very like it, was doubtless the first act of that noble enterprise by which Christian light and truth were made in this island the potent dispellers of heathen darkness. And where, in all the island, could a sweeter, sunnier spot be found than that which the Garrison vale presents?

At the distant period we speak of the dew of the world's youth was still upon its insular meadows, and the joyous carolling of song-birds filled the air with melodies aa fresh as they were primeval. Here then, if a choice of situation were granted to him, the pioneer missionary would construct his little church of wattles, and teach the rude clansmen of the island to resort to it daily for prayer and praise. In due time a school would follow, civilisation would advance, and the triumphs of Christianity know no bounds.

OTHER ANCIENT CROSSES

In the cemetery of the Cathedral and Collegiate Church there are other two ancient crosses, and also a portion of the shaft of a third-making four all counted. One of these crosses has a considerable resemblance to No.2, plate 74 of "The Stones of Scotland." No. 8, on the same plate, . evidently represents the incised cross on the porphyry boulder. The former of these shows an incised cross of the star-fish pattern within an enclosing double-ring. It may be called the Double-ringed Cross. It is only a fragment, but fortunately the circular-headed portion of the cross is preserved intact, as well as a considerable part of the shaft. A very fine specimen of an ancient cross it is : indeed, it is quite a gem. Chiselled out of a slab of fair white sandstone, the length of the existing portion is about 25 inches, the diameter of the circular head is It inches, the width of the shaft (four inches below the circular head) is 8½ inches, and the thickness is about 3½. Upon the shaft of the cross, and under the circular head, there is another incised figure of a cross standing on a crescent, and bearing a-top another crescent. The higher of the two crosses shows six ovals, six angular parts between the ovals, and another series of ovals within the encircling rings.

The Porphyry Cross, as it may be called, is an incised cross, cut upon the flat face or surface of a much abraded or water-worn boulder. The boulder is either whinstone or hard porphyry, is of a roundish or somewhat disk-like form, but slightly convex on the unsculptured face. It is 15 inches along its greatest diameter by 12 inches across that line, and its thickness is nearly 7 inches. It was found, nearly thirty years ago, somewhere between the Garrison and St. Andrew's Church.

The third fragment is a portion of the shaft of a ornamented cross, but it is very difficult to decipher the design, and to determine whether the decoration is interlacing knotwork or something like a hawk or deer.

It is of white sandstone, and has two parallel incised lines or grooves running along one side of the shaft, but no similar lines can be perceived near the other verge. This interesting fragment is 18 inches in length, as measured over the space between those two points of the stone which are farthest apart ; its width is 7¼¼ inches, and its thickness 3¼¼. In order to distinguish this cross, the writer suggests that it be called the Falcon-cross.

We have it on the highest authority that there are crosses of a Cornish type in the island, and our double-ringed cross may be safely referred to that category. Referring to certain similar ancient crosses at St. Blane's Church in the island of Bute, Dr. John Stuart says :- "The crosses here represented stand on the south side of the burying-ground [of said church.] The character of the circular-headed stones, having a cross figured within the circle, and with a short shaft or set on a short pillar, corresponds with those of Cumbrae. Many of the Cornish crosses resemble this class of monument . . .

Crosses of the same character are found in some of the old churches of the Isle of Man, but they are not considered to be of Norse origin, as most of the Manx crosses are."-Sculpt.Stones of Scot.,ii. 37.

The similarity between Cornish and Irish crosses is very striking, and seems clearly to show that many early preachers of Hibernian birth visited Cornwall in order to propagate the true faith. A similar zeal, on the part of these and their brother missionaries, brought their benign influence to bear upon the western islands of Scotland.

One of the crosses at the college-the Porphyry Cross-bears a marked resemblance to the cross which is seen on the tomb of (?) Bishop Patrick, and who died in Iona, A.D. 1174.

At Millburn House, a few years ago, the writer saw several other interesting examples of these ancient Cumbrae crosses, and with reference to these his note-book indicates (1) a flat, thin piece of sandstone with interlacing knotwork on it, evidently a fragment of a cross; (2) a fine specimen, having a couple of doves standing in the upper angles of the cross, each of them apparently engaged pruning her feathers ; while the two quarters underneath the cross-arms are occupied with an endless three-fold loop supposed by some to symbolise the Holy Trinity. It is scarcely necessary to state here what the sacred symbol of the holy Dove imports. . . . . A small segment of this cross has been broken off ; (3) another circular-headed stone with a cross chiselled in relief upon it, and within the circular rim four marks which, along with one in the centre, are supposed to represent the five wounds of the CRUCIFIED ONE.

About five-and-twenty years ago these crosses were received from the then minister of the parish-Rev. A. Marshall-by the late John Levack, Esq., who informed the writer of these pages that he [Levack] knew where these crosses were found, viz., in the ancient churchyard at Kirktoun of Cumbrae.

They were left at the manse by the Rev. James Drummond, who knew them to be crosses which had been found, at different times, by the sexton while engaged in digging graves in the old churchyard. For two of the ancient crosses at "God's Acre," by the Collegiate Church, a similar origin may be confidently claimed.

Exact or definite information as to these two is lacking, but their close similarity of type and character lends strong support to the view that they also were found at the old ecclesiastical site.
We close the section with a

LIST OF THE CLERGY
OF THE
CATHEDRAL AND COLLEGIATE CHURCH.

PROVOST.-Right Rev. Alex. Chinnery-Haldane, Bishop of Argyll and the Isles.

CANONS.-Very Rev. R. G. Mapleton, M.A., Dean of Argyll and the Isles, and Incumbent of Kilmartin ; Rev. J. A. Ewing, M.A., Rector of Westmill ; Rev. H. Brown, Rector of Long Stratton ; Rev. J. R.- Dakers, Incumbent of St. Andrew's, Cumbrae.

HON. CANONS.-Rev. G. C. White, M.A., Vicar of Newland and Warden of Beauchamp Alms-houses ; Hon. and Rev. H. Douglas, Vicar of St. Paul's, Worcester; Rev. W. Bright, D.D., Canon of Christ Church, Oxford, and Reg. Professor of Ecclesiastical History; Rev. W. Bell, Forbes Librarian, Edinburgh, and Chapter Clerk of Cumbrae; Rev. H. Meynell, M.A., Vicar of Denstone; Rev. D. MacColl, Incumbent of Fort William; Rev. R. G. Weldon, M.A., Incumbent of Rothesay; Rev. A. J. Maclean, M.A, Priest on Mission to Nestorian Church.

PRIEST IN CHARGE.-Rev. C. W. Worlledge.

(5) KAMES AND FERRY-ROAD

We begin with South Kames, on the lands of which the Newtown was built. The houses of this portion of the burgh of Millport line the shore road immediately to the east of the Garrison, and command a free unobstructed view of the picturesque bay, the islets, and the mainland. The superior character of the buildings, and the variety manifested in height, tint, and architectural features, combine to give a decided aspect of grace and beauty to the whole length of this handsome row.

Of a morning when the summer's sun pours its flood of light over the sands in front of the houses, and blandest airs from the south just touch the waters of the bay,-making a "cat's paw" here and there, -and the sweet freshness of the 'caller' tangle and seaweed at the ebb comes filtering through the air like a breath of purest ozone, -in such circumstances it is truly the height of enjoyment to have an early walk along the marine esplanade, and take casual notice of whatever most interests the eye.

No less pleasant is it at eventide, especially when the great full moon rises red and glowing like a world of fire right over the Eagle's Crag, and lays a lane of bright golden light along the shimmering sea all the way from the Leac [lecque] to the

Farland shore. Such an impressive spectacle was witnessed the other evening by numerous parties walking along the fore-shores or strolling on the sands, and several of them were heard to say they had never before seen such a beautiful sight.

Standing on the esplanade (in front of Allan's shop and clock) one sees the Allen-islets in front, numerous little boats and yawls anchored over the Rigg-a submarine bank extending from the nearer islet to the sands of Garrison-bay-and, somewhat towards the left front, the little, handy pier for small boats, which has for generations been called the Leac. Moving eastwards along the esplanade one passes, on the right, the rocky ledges of sandstone and comes, opposite the Free Church, to a little rocky "wick," or creek, now called Flisswick, or the creek of the flagstone ledges.

The large house in front stretching right across the greater part of the green esplanade is called Crosshouse, and right over the ridge of its roof we have the south end of innean Brae, clad with a tall and thriving wood. Close behind the last-named brae of declivity (and on the hill-top) is the place called Lots-Barreil, meaning the lots or plots of tilled ground near the verge or brink of Barreil, i.e., the cliff-top. This place is easily reached by going up the pass of Corn-ballach, the stile for which is opposite the gate of Provost Brown's nursery-gardens.

Speaking of this cliff-top reminds one of the fact that the vale at the foot of it bears the old name of Speannil-dale, from a word signifying a steep slope, a declivity. As already mentioned, Innean-brae alias Ninian-brae is the other or alternative appellation for projecting bluff of which, not many years ago, stood a tall flagstaff right over the gilt weather-vane of Kames House.

The view of Cumbrae Bay from the elevated summit of the bluff crag just referred to is one of the most beautiful to be had in this wide world. Early should the visitor strive to imprint upon the tablets of his memory the surpassing loveliness of the scene which is beheld from the top of Barreil.

If it be in the morning hour, he will see it to the best advantage, for, With the sun behind Him, and its glorious light falling upon the varied and picturesque panorama, he can gaze with undazzled eye upon the charming features of the bay, survey at leisure the blue waters of the firth beyond the Lorne dotted over with swiftly-moving "liners" and other stately ships, scan the grey cliffs and green slopes of Kelspoke in Bute, and take in at a glance the soul-stirring picture of Arran's majestic peaks and dark deep-bosomed corries. Here is a slight sketch of the Arran Fells as seen from our island in early morning :- Came the morning robed in light, and hung her banner out above the gateways of the day. Her earliest beam smote the trident peak of Kead Vol. Presently there came another and at once, like a fairy clothed with light, went a-searching through the crevice on the forehead of the Fell.

Then another and another in quick succession came, and without a moment's delay, began peering into the clefts and crannies which scar the shoulder of the mountain. Soon a great troop of these Light-elves was busy at work, exploring every nook and corrie, lesser spike and pinnacle ; while every one of them was happier than another at having found a pretty thing to brighten up, and make once more visible to mortals.

If any of the latter class of beings had been early astir, they would have seen not only the arrival of the bright little fellows, and the many little gems of light-and-pencil sketches which they first dashed off on face of sky and fell, but they would also have witnessed the splendid scenic effect which, in the next instance, their fine artistic touches harmoniously created.-Landmarks, p. 228.

Those who take pleasure in philological studies will find in the Cumbraes" great store of interesting local names. Many of them are of Celtic origin, but perhaps quite as many are of Norse or Lowland Scots. Innean-brae, for example, is pure Gaelic, and yet, it can scarcely be doubted that the first part of the compound is a loan word from the old Teutonic tongue of the Norsemen,- old Danish enni, Swedish einni, the modern form of which is panna, meaning the forehead, the brow. and metaphorically a steep declivity or bluff. With s prefixed this term gives us "speann," as in Witharspuin, meaning the wooded steep or brae-face. It also give us Spennymoor and other local names in which the compounds are purely Teutonic. From it wee also have "spindrift," that is, the drift or spray from the brow or ridge of the foam-flecked billow.

Ninian Brae is the other form of Innean-brae, and is exactly the same Gaelic word, with this mark or difference, that the former has a fragment of the Gaelic definite article (an) adhering to it or coalescing with it. This is what happens not unfrequently, even in the Lowland-Scots tongue; for we say nickname where we mean "an eke name." Our Ninian Brae and Ninian Park have, therefore, no connection in the world with this honoured name of St. Ninian, the great apostle of the Southern Picts, and who, possibly enough, may have been the very first Christian missionary to step ashore and preach the everlasting Gospel to the ancient Picts of Cumbrae.

We know that the Picts were here in the sixth and seventh centuries, but in the Venerable Bede's time the Angli had come in on them, and they were then considered to be in the province of

Bernicia.-Reeves, p. 294. Bede was writing about the year 715, just 30 years after that fatal day on which the fiery Picts made it complete end of King Ecgfrith and his Northumbrian host.

One result of this decisive defeat of the Anglian power was the immediate departure of Trumwin, "the man of God," and his clerks from Abercorn, and their rapid retreat to Whitby. Now as Abercorn is about midway between the Cumbraes and Dunbar, to which latter town the fame of St. Beya of the Little Cumbrae reached, it is likely enough that these events restored the Picts once more to full power iu the Cumbraes, and thus gave St. Beya a better prospect of being left undisturbed in her island-retreat.

Let us now (in thought at least) return to our station by the shore of Flisswick, and to the esplanade in front of the Free Church. Looking towards the Farland-point one sees successively Lucky's Bight, or the cove of the water demon that strews the place with entangling "partan-strings;" the Minister's Rock with the little creek, called Port-loy, or the prior's port ; then the lofty red crags of Craiganiller or the eagle's cliff; then the cosy little cave designated Gipsy-cave, and next the remainder of the range of red-rock precipices.

Kames Bay lies under these picturesque cliffs, and even extends far enough inland to come under the shadow of the much-wooded Ninian Brae. The grandest-looking brow on the whole western face of these cliffs was, unfortunately, undermined by the only too enterprising quarrymen and came down bodily in the dark, one fine morning, with a fearful crash ; and, had it not been that the mountain's brow slid away downwards rather than toppled over, the results would have been very disastrous. As it was, a sore disfigurement of the towering rock-face was the worst injury done, but the kindly hand of Time has hung her green and flower-embroidered drapery over the scaur, and another generation has grown up to whom the old features of Whinny-Heugh (as it was called) are as a dream of the night.

Let us now advance a little more rapidly, keeping to the promenade on the seaward side of Crosshouse. Lang-point is the name of the rocky ness or point on the right and which, as seen from the hill-top to the east, presents an appearance exactly like the outstretched wing of a falcon.

On its rocky ledges sit the solitary heron of a morning, just when the dim "greyking" is merging into the dawn ; and when the gates of day have been thrown just a little more ajar, there may often be seen, out in the bay, quite a flock of sea-gulls flying sportively about and feeding on the shoals of innumerable syle. Sometimes, too, a school of porpoises have a swimming match around the island for days together, and may be heard puffing and blowing as those who strive to be first at the winning-post.

Crosshouse being turned, and the second seat beyond it reached, we have on the left the tree-clad eminence of Barrheads, on which stands the fine old villa of Craigenross, long occupied by the Misses Carmichael. Advancing about sixty yards, we have, on the left, the site of Trahorque, a winter pool or lakelet now represented by the gardens of Kelburne-place ; and next, about as many yards more in advance, the opening of Woodland-street, through a portion of which ran the Leny-burn [lenny-burn] across the green into the west nook of the closely adjacent bay.

Pass along in front of Devonport-place, and in ninety-two paces from its western end reach Park-house on the left, and enter immediately upon Ferry Road. Kameshay villas and those of Marine Parade are on the right. Taking about thirty paces from Parkhouse, and going along the Ferry-road, we reach a walk or avenue, on the left, which may well be called Leny-burn Avenue, because it leads right up to the field or meadow through which the pure water of Leny rivulet still flows. Turning up this avenue and leaving Beverley-cottage on the right, we come in eighty paces from Ferry-road to the Nursery wicket, and about one hundred paces more, in advance, brings us to the villa named Kameston House. Going forward in the same direction for about another hundred paces, we come to the stone dike or wall, on the left, which encloses the held in which the Gas Works stand. If we may enter the lea-field which lies on the north side of this stone wall, and proceed west for some twenty paces, we shall find ourselves by the flowery brink of the dear old brook of Leny-burn, and hear its purling music as it wimples through the meadow.

Not for nothing has this little bit of an Itinerary been so carefully given. To let the interested visitor see the site of the ancient hamlet of Kames,-this has been one of the main reasons for troubling him with these minute directions.

Having crossed Leny-burn let the visitor go right up the slope towards the west, and he will come, in about a minute of time, to the salient, out-standing, and highly-uplifted crag which we now call Altar Rock. Not that any one, to-day at least, really believes it to have been used as an altar ; but the late W. Keddie, Esq., appears to have received from some of the older inhabitants some hint or suggestion of this idea, for in a certain paper, read before a learned Society, he speaks of religious rites having been traditionally associated with this prominent rock. The writer, however, has no hesitation in rejecting this representation and regarding it as a mere fancy, even although in his Landmarks (p. 90, under the name of Trohork) he calls attention to the fact that the old Norse word horg signifies a group of stones for sacrificial rites, a stone group or altar.

Jamieson, speaking a few years ago, remembered the ruins of five crofters' houses belonging to this old hamlet of Kames, and which houses stood at a little distance from the Gasworks. The cottages represented by these ruins, and a few more of the old crofters' houses, extended along the Leny-burn nearly to the Breckoch farm-steading. A circle of ash-trees pointed out the former position of a cluster of these old cottages and the kailyards attached to them. These aged ash-trees were cut down by the woodman's axe about the year 1820, but thirty-six years earlier (in 1784) the crofters began to receive allotments of ground on the shore lands of South Kames, where cottages were built, and thus the Newtoun of Kames (now included in the burgh of Millport) came into existence.

In the year 1805 there were only five or six cottages in this new town or village. They were of one storey only, and were thatched with straw. It is known that these crofters, or kindly tenants, built the cottages at their own expense; but it is also certain that their neighbours lent a helping hand in fetching stones and timber for building materials. Of "heather-and-dub" cottages not one such has ever been heard of in the island, and all these cottages were built of the beautiful, fine-tinted stone which is ao plentiful in the neighbourhood.

Some of the original Newtoun feus were taken up by the mate and second mate of "the King's cutter," which made the anchorage at the Allens her rendezvous or chief station. Several of the seamen on board the same vessel also acquired feus. Hunter was the mate, or chief petty officer ; and Cunningham was second mate. Archibald Maconachie, whose father was the piper on board "the Cumraes Cutter," was one of the seamen who had an allotment, and built a cottage upon it. But the first of these cottages to be built was the third east of the Garrison, and it was erected by Paterson, mason and contractor. A few artisans also acquired sites, and did their best for themselves and for the little community.

It may be held as pretty certain that several of the old Cumbrae families are descendants of the Brandanes who fought so bravely at the Battle of the Standard, and also at that of Falkirk, in the time of "Wallace wight," under the Stout Stewart of Bute. Now these Brandanes have evidently received their name from beorn, a hero, a warrior, a "baron." By valour and strength of arm every man of them won his sword-land, and by his good sword he kept it against all comers. As in the "Song of the Outlaw Murray," the old Brandane, by altering a word, might say-

Thir lands o' Cumra's Isle so fair,
I wan them from the enemie;
Like as I wan them, sae will I keep them,
Contrair a' kings in Christentie.

It was this spirit of daring and stern resolve to preserve their freedom that made these Cumbrae "barons" or Brandanes what they were- men good at need, ready at a moment's notice to buckle on their armour and march out shoulder to shoulder against the foe. Did the Haisill-beacon on the Farland blaze up of an evening, or Goudenbury-hill shoot its warning gleam over the sea, then was the mustering of the warrior-barons, and a stiff dispute with any foolhardy marauders who might venture to face them. In this sense the barons of Cumbrae were barons or Brandanes indeed. In other words, they were warriors and heroes, and being such they were of old called barons. But "barons" in the modern sense, as holding land in feudal dependence upon a superior lord, they were not.

Having cleared the way by these explanations, we may now speak freely of the "barony of the Hill"-long held by the Hunters,-of other old baronies which tradition tells us of, -and of Baron Macfee of the Breaghogh. Waddell, writing about forty years ago, says that a descendant of the "baron of the hill" (or Torr-mor) was then alive in the island, but he does not mention his name.

The name of this " last of the barons" can, however, be given, for a few of the older natives still remember old Isaac Hunter of The Hill. Baron Macfee figures largely in the fire-side tales of the islanders. He is said to, have been tied to a tree and put to death in a most savage manner by a party of reiving kernes (caterans) from Cowal. These ruthless marauders carried of, on the baron's flails, the well-filled sacks of corn which were stored up in his barn.

His son, however, made good his escape, slashing of with his sword the legs of a sleuth-hound that was sent after him, and gaining eventually the security of a den-still called Macfee's Cave-on the eastern side of Heatheren-keipel Dyke. This den, or hiding-place, has been formed by huge masses of rock which have fallen from the adjacent cliff and it may yet be discovered at a distance of ninety paces east of the great dyke just mentioned.

Another episode falls to be introduced here. It is the pitiful and yet picturesque story of Esmé Stewart, the disinherited duke of Lennox, who found a retreat "in the cold Scots winter" in our little island some three centuries ago. Often may he have received the kindly hospitality of the villagers of Kames, and he who basked so lately in the sunshine of the young King's smiles, and rose with meteor-like speed to the glory of a Scottish dukedom, with lands in every one of ten countries, was now well content, stripped as he was of his honours and possessions, to sit by the board of some humble peasant, and share the common fare of the household. But this poor wanderer was not even allowed to remain long in the island, for his place of refuge being discovered, he had "to move farther from danger into the remote highland fastness of Cowal."-See Burton's Hist. of Scot., v. 426, 455.

These lands were held by the Hunters of Paltreath or Hunterston at a period dating as far back as three centuries ago. Patrick Huntar was served heir, in the year 1617, to the five-pound land of old extent of South Keames, in the island of Mekle Cumray. Hunter of that ilk was forester in heritage of the lesser Cumbrae, it being of old a royal deer park ; and this same family, in virtue of their forestry rights, maintained their claim to the peregrine falcons bred on the red farland-crag.

Robert Allan, when a mere stripling, was lowered by a rope over this crag, and, in spite of the fierce attack of the parent-birds, succeeded in taking from the nest three fine young "gem (game) hawks," one of which was long kept at Portrye. This daring exploit was enacted about sixty years ago ; and it is said that the tame falcon, if a mouse were chucked into the air before it, would instantly make a rapid swoop and seize the little victim ere it reached the ground.

Retracing our steps by the way we came, and re-entering upon the Ferry-road, we pass, on the right, the homestead of what was formerly Kames-mill, where the carles and kindly tenants used to have their corn "multure." In earlier times the handmill was used by the inhabitants, and not a few querns remain in the island to attest the fact. Speannil-dale is on the right and is partly occupied with villas and gardens.

A little farther on, one comes to the Nursery-gate, opposite to which there is a stile leading into the wood and up the sloping pass of Corn-ballach to the brow of the hill, where the grand prospect may be enjoyed at leisure. Keeping at present, however, to the road, and leaving the stile behind, one comes in about six or eight minutes to the branch road, on the left, leading over to the farmhouse of Ballykellet. By the way one sees the Maiden Knowe in front of the farmhouse, and a little farther to the west, the fine green eminences called Gouards-hill, or the hill of the manorhouse. Still further to the west-north-west are the two eminences called Tarraigh, and to the south-west of these we have Play-hill and the Shighans.

The last mentioned of these local names signifies the mounts of the fairy-folk, and is a manifest survival of the old superstition which tenanted each pretty green eminence with ban-shees, making a "seely-court" of it, that is, the court of the happy people. Play-hill rises boldly from the upper side of Fauld Makneansh, and it is very remarkable that this latter name undoubtedly means the field of the gathering or of the fair.

The "fair" was surely held on the anniversary of some saint's day, and both of these local names point unmistakably to the games and sports which the people of old were wont to indulge in on festival days.

Maiden Knowe, regarded as a name, probably refers to similar annual gathering or assembly, and in this case we may have a trace or indication of the honour paid to the lady-missionary Maura, who is presumably the virgin-saint of the island (see page 8). Barbay, or the yellow hill, is also seen, and it forms the sky-line to the north-west of the farmhouse.

Glen-touthar, or the glen of the chieftain's estate, is the thickly-Wooded glen to the north of the farmhouse-steading, and its fine euphonious name clearly points to the ancient baron or lord of Ballykellet. His Hall or residence, if planted originally on the same spot as that occupied, until 1836, by the mansion-house of Sir Robert Montgomerie, commanded a charming prospect of sea and vale, and was well sheltered from the rough east winds by a protecting line of tree-clad heights.

It eventually had its name from some ancient chapel or cell of devotion, but whether the primary reference was to Cullyleyne (the nun's oratory), or to some primitive Culdee chapel, it were hard to determine. The subject is one which scarcely admits of further discussion here, but those who are interested in such questions will find a fuller account of this one in the author's Landmarks.

To find the exact position of the baronet's old mansion-house of Ballykellet, let the inquirer take seventy paces along the side-road leading to farm-house of the same name, and he will come to a small ash-tree on the left, which, along with an aged bour-tree a few paces further on, marks the site of the garden wall. About a stone-cast south of these two trees stood the mansion or manor-house of the Montgomeries, surrounded by grand old ash-trees, the hewing down of which was witnessed by some of the Kames "callants" who are still alive. Here the Montgomeries dwelt for generations, and truly they had in possession a delightful heritage.

From father to son passed this heritage until, as a property, it fell by inheritance to the baronet of Skelmorlie, the heir of a kindred house. Combining the two properties, the insular and that of the mainland, the Montgomerie had means enough whereby to live as a gentleman of high degree, and doubtless the courtyard of their island-hall often rang to the clarion-call of the trumpeter of Kames-not to arms perhaps, but to the scarcely less stirring episodes of the hunting field. Patron of the "parish kirk," owner of "a peice (sic) of kirkland" and also of "the King's lands" in this locality, he would have in his day a position of much influence, and we trust that he used it in the interest of his retainers' welfare.

His shield, or escutcheon, deftly cut out in one entire stone surmounted the door of the old parish church, and the interesting old relic may be seen to this day in the garden wall of the manse. Its genuineness is sealed by Drummond's testimony, by the presence of the three fleurs-des-lis, the three annulets, the motto Garde Bien and the names of Sir Robert Montgomery and Dame Margrat (sic) Douglas.

It is nearly a couple of centuries since this Sir Robert, the last male heir, came into possession of this property of Over-cames or Ballykellet. How long he enjoyed his patrimony is a matter that may be left to the genealogists, but in the course of time his fertile lands in this fairest of dales passed by purchase into the hands of the Earl of Glasgow, where they still remain. It is a record of change and ever-shifting destinies. Gone from their island-home and fair possessions are all the Cumbrae descendants of the hero of Otterbourne!

As we think of the brave knights and fair ladies, who with their retainers and yeomen friends used to meet on this sunny slope and go out with the royal birds for a day's hawking, we cannot but feel a deep sense of regret that the old hall or mansion of Ballykellet was not spared to become (as in that event it would) a picturesque old ruin, its tall peel-tower clad with "ivy green," and its grand old ash-trees casting a pleasant shade in summer, or in winter's blast sighing out the old refrain, "Cha till mi tuilleadh" (I return no more).

Retracing our steps to the Ferry-road, and having reached it, notice immediately on the right four steps, which lead into a path through the wood and onto the farmhouse of Craigengour. This path skirts the edge of a deep dingle or little glen called Auld-goute [gote], a name which may be interpreted the dell of devotion, the glen of prayer. About twenty paces from the head of this picturesque little glen, and at the foot of a shaded mossy rock of considerable height, there is a cool and copious fountain called Buttar Well, that is, the bidder-well or the wishing well. Martin tells us that "this island has a chappel (sic) and a well which the natives esteem a catholicon for all diseases."

Of this healing-well the writer has never otherwise heard, but he holds that there are good reasons for identifying it with the Buttar-well or well of the petitioners. Cryslan-well, or the health-giving fountain, is in Bute, and is one of those clear little basins of pure spring-water which were formerly much resorted to by pilgrim devotees. Arran has a similar well, the long Gaelic name of which signifies the well of the country-folk's superstitious usages, and points to the healing benefits, real or imaginary, which were believed to reside in its waters.

Kintyre, too, has a well of like reputation, and near to it are the slight but distinct remains of a tiny oratory or sacellum, which the Norse settlers called Leil-veit, that is, the tiny temple, oratory, or sanctuary. In this last instance there can be no doubt about the oratory, for the well in its near vicinity was called Vey-kell or the chapelspring. Now, since the Bute well referred to has a ruined chapel (capellula) stood somewhere in the vicinity of the Buttar-well. The conclusion is one which receives a large amount of additional support from other local facts, the full exposition of which cannot be introduced here. It may only be added that this little spring under the mossy fern-clad rock may have been one of those fountains which "foolish people worshipped" so late as the time of Charles the Great.

During the prevalence of heathen rites certain fountains were objects of veneration, and the paying of vows at such places was more or less practised by the barbarians in Christian times. The clergy maintained a perpetual warfare against the worship of trees, fountains, and certain stones, "as if any divinity (numen) resided there capable of conferring good or evil.

CRAIGLEE

is the next point of interest, as we advance northward, but the Dripping-rock o' Craigielea exists now only as a sadly marred and exploited trap-dyke. The exigences of recent road-making, or rather the widening of the road from Allt-goute to the Ferryroad, sealed the doom of this well-known landmark and picturesque crag. An inauspicious day saw the work of destruction begun, and very soon the whole front of the hoary moss-clad rock was hewn down and transformed into "dasses" or heaps of mere road-metal. It was surely a deed done in haste, but for it there is no place of repentance. It was of a piece with the previous hewing down of the high picturesque rocks which adorned the Covans-shore and the Leac. The utilitarian spirit has its triumphs, and shows them in many of the improvements which have recently been effected within the bounds of the burgh ; but one would fain hope that, for the future, our trim little island shall be spared the loss of any more of its interesting natural objects, and that its many well-wishers shall have the pleasure of seeing every one of its picturesque features preserved.

Gouklan Wood and its ancient "Stannin-stane" now engages our attention for a brief space. The nearest corner of this wood (on the right) is about two hundred and thirty paces from the Dripping-rock, and close to this corner or angle of the wood is Craiglee-yett, or the gate which secures the branch road leading to the homestead of Craigengour.

Having entered the wood at the near corner, and taking pains to make as little trespass as possible, let the visitor who wishes to scan the hoary features of this fine specimen of the ancient "rude stone monuments," proceed nearly due east to a point fifteen paces from the eastern verge of the wood, and thirty paces from the south wall or boundary of the wood. Here he will find the ancient pillar-stone-the Gouklan Pillar-standing about seven feet above the soil and presenting, towards the top, a broad breast, more than three spans in width. Looked at from the south-west it is seen tapering downwards, deeply scored and ribbed by the weathering of ages, and sprinkled all over with thriving grey lichens.

One cannot look upon it in the sombre quiet atmosphere of the wood without feeling that it is a really fine old monument, and worthy in every way to be carefully guarded and conserved. The stone of which the venerable monument is composed is a hard, close-grained, white sandstone. It stands on a somewhat elevated plain, which, however, is but a "ballach" or pass leading from Kames to Balloch-bay.

At the base or foot of the pillar lie three large boulders, another a little farther off and four others about four yards to the east. As to its name not much can be said here, but it is extremely probable that it signifies the Pictish pillar-stone ; in other words, the standing stone of the Selgovae. Coutsnouth is a very remarkable stronghold or fenced town near the Border, and as its name signifies the Yeats' fortress it has (in its first syllable) a close analogy to the name of out pillar in the wood.

Cumbrae up till a recent date possessed a good many more of these rude upright stones. They stood in the pleasant vale near to the house of Baron Macfee of Braighagh, and a line of twelve or more pillar-stones stretched from the garden of the present homestead to a distance of fully one hundred yards southward.

One of them (standing lately in the garden) was a fine obelisk of white conglomerate, nearly seven feet in height above the soil ; another at or near the south end of the line still stands nearly five feet above the ground, and only a few yards from the latter a third column, sixty-six inches in length, lay prostrate. They were evidently set up, in ancient times, to mark the sepulchre of one or more distinguished men-chiefs or princes, or heroes or renown. Braighagh indeed, regarded as a local name, may well be interpreted the burial-mound of the champions-brugh athaich.

Druidical theories in connection with these ancient monuments have been utterly scotched. Recent investigations by means of the spade and a true scientific philology have given the finishing stroke to such manifest absurdities. Dr. Reeves makes short work of the silly tales vended in Iona about "the never-failing Druids," and without hesitation he characterises them as fiction, imperfect fiction, nonsense.

Our grandfathers often spoke of Peaghts and warriors in connection with cairns, camps and standing stones, but the writer has yet to learn that tradition (that prince of liars) ever taught them to speak of Druids in the same connection. They were altogether innocent of tales about "Druids sacrificing their bleeding victims" on alter stones till the followers of Jones and Stukely began to disseminate their fanciful doctrines among the peasantry and others.

There was, however, another class of tales which gave a popular interest to the cairns and other sepulchral monuments. These were the tales about the hidden treasures which they were believed to contain, and which, in actual fact, have not unfrequently been discovered. Taken along with the stories which represented the cairns as the resting-places of the mighty dead, these tales evidently constituted the staple of our forefathers' conversation regarding them.

Sometimes it was "a cog of gold" that was reported to be lying deep within the grave-mound, and was there for digging for. At other times, or in other counties, it was "a bowie fu' o' gowd" (a tubful of gold) that constituted the cairn-treasure.

Bute shows us a portion of an ancient monument in the form of three great rude pillar-stones, and the old Gaelic name of these massive

117

columns signifies the ruin of the sepulchre of the Celtic lord. Did space permit. many parallel examples might be adduced, but it must suffice to say that, after careful and prolonged investigations of these ancient standing stones as well as of their names, the writer has been led to the conclusion that they mark the last resting-places of the great or mighty dead-heroes, chiefs, and rulers.

Taking a final glance at the stately old pillar in the wood, stained and freckled as it is with the lichen-tints of age, we may be permitted briefly to state that other two pillars are reported to have been closely associated with it. Jamieson and others dug a circle of pits around the existing stone, but no ancient relics or remains were found. Doubtless they had been too late-anticipated by the treasure-seekers-or had somehow failed to use the spade at the proper place.

Retracing our path through the plantation, we presently regain the main road. Taking a few steps in advance, we have on the left a belt of wood, and beyond it Druimskillin, or the hill-ridge of the tiny chapel. The name of this ridge evidently refers to Cullyleyne, or the Nun's oratory, close by. Cullyleyne is the name of the second field to the west of the road, and along the east side of this field there flows a little rivulet in which the peasants used to steep their lint. The Nun's Oratory (an undoubted discovery) appears to have stood near to this rivulet and close to the north boundary of the field but outside of it.

The site of this ancient or primitive cell may probably be justly identified with certain remains on a somewhat rough spot or mound, near the north-east corner of the said field, but outside of it a few yards.

A fit retreat it would be for the "grey nun" or anchoret, who-to win the crown of sanctity-longed to secure such a solitude, and to build for herself in the heart of it a lodge of devotion. The wild heathery uplands and the rocky peaked-hills, of monny-mor (great hill-moor) close in the view on the west and north, but a splendid prospect towards the south would always be available.

Beyond these hills, and at no great distance from the western shore of the island, were two or three more of these cells of austerity. They were probably built in the course of the seventh or eighth century, and may have been long in use prior to the advent of the northern sea-rovers. Annat-ydras, or the chapel of penitence, stood on the lands of Skermorlie.

And so early as the fifth century "the devout virgin Crumtherim lived in a stone oratory near Armagh." Penance-hill is near the chief old ecclesiastical site of the island, and we know that St. Beya spent the latter portion of her life as an anchoret in the solitude of Little Cumbrae.

There is nothing more of absorbing interest along the remainder of the road to the Ferry-house, and as the whole of this road is such a favourite walk with the young people, we may now, upon conditions, leave it very much to themselves. the only terms or conditions are summed up in a request for time to add a very few closing sentences by way of an Itinerary.

Passing onwards, then, the traveller comes, in another quarter of a mile, to the branch road on the left which leads round Tonnal-hill, or the hill of the gathering, to the farmhouse of Figatch, where permission to explore the romantic beauties of Gawns-glen will be readily granted. Glead Stane, the highest point or peak in Isle of Cumbrae, may be reached in five or ten minutes "O'er hill and holt, and moor and fen," from any local point on this so-called branch road.

A walk of about two hundred yards farther along our main road brings one to the branch road, on the left, which leads over to the farmhouse of Portrye, near which is the old barony of Ballycown.

The two latter places are near White-bay (see p. 20). Keeping by the main road, the farmhouse of Ballochmartin is reached in two or three minutes more. Holding on our way past this farmhouse, and traversing nearly a mile of the road beyond it, we come to the Ferryhouse at foot of Doun-craig, and close by the new Pier of "Balloch."

CHAPTER III

KIRKTOUN OF CUMBRAE

The old ecclesiastical site merits special attention. Any one who has persued the foregoing pages will be in some measure prepared to realise the early importance of what was evidently the chief of the ancient Cumbrae churches.

The interesting old crosses which have been found in the soil of the ancient churchyard at Kirktoun, and which have already been described, will have led him to perceive that a thriving Christian community, well advanced in many of the arts which civilisation implies, dwelt in the pleasant vale around the precincts of a sixth or seventh century church.

Perhaps we will presently find that there are good reasons for assigning an even earlier date to the first planting of a church in the island. If Ninian, the great apostle of the southern Picts, was privileged (as we know he was) about the year 410 to consecrate a churchyard at Glasgow, and if there was a bishop "exercising his office " in Scotland as early as the year 314, we may well believe that Ninian himself was not likely to miss the Cumbraes on his way through Kyle, nor the oppertunity of preaching the gospel to the indwellers thereof.

If he was the earliest pioneer missionary to land on the island-shore, his name and labours were sufficiently remembered to cause a small chapel to be reared in his honour towards the eastern side of the island. The efforts he made in the training of the youth proved the happy means of raising up a goodly band of earnest disciples, who pressed forward into fresh districts, unfurling the banner of the Cross, and acting as the victorious vanguard of a noble succession of Christian pastors and teachers.

One or more of these would remain in the island, doing duty in the school and the higher departments of the institution, as well as in the church. If any chief of the church old Damnian race of Firbolgs still held his ground and his clan in the isle, we can, according to well-known parallels, imagine Ninian or one of his companions doing what Columba and Drostan did at Deer-- asking of the chief a piece of ground whereon to build a sanctuary or house of prayer.

The request granted, forewith arose the holy fane. It might be, at first, a mere creel- house, that is, a house framed of stakes or wattles with interlacing knot-work of willow-wands. But very soon a church of stone would be erected, and in those early days of missionary enterprise it would be not merely a church, but a church combined with a Christian institution for the instruction of the natives, the doors of which would be open to all.

When the husbandman had committed his seed to the furrows he would choose a season of comparative leisure in order to obtain for himself some instruction within the walls of the institution. And when the harvest was gathered in he would find another opportunity of enjoying a similar benefit. Nor would the warrior-chief himself be disobedient to the divine invitation. At any rate, it often happened that he was not. These old Yeats or Picts were too strong-witted and sensible to permit themselves to hesitate between candid inquiry and stolid indifference.

As a result of this spirit the hardy Pict laid aside his spear and listened to the teachings of those men whose weapons of warfare were not carnal, but mighty withal to the pulling down of strongholds.

The high places of heathenism were purged and consecrated to a purer worship; the diviners and magicians felt their influence on the wane, and, like Coifi, œ were sometimes the foremost to renounce it altogether. When the aged veterans of the Cross had fulfilled their task, native teachers and ministers stepped into their places and carried on the good work which they had begun.

Doubtless the clergy were aggressive, and took pains to reach those who might not come to them. In obedience to the spirit of this holy aggressiveness they went out to the people. They would visit them in their queer little conical huts of wattle or wicker-work; they would visit the court or lys of the chieftain, and they would tell them all in kindly tones of the folly of demon-worship, and of the beauty and excellence of the Christian Faith.

By these and other means the great and noble work would be carried on successfully, and often through long years of unbroken peace. At times there might be war or other disturbing interruptions, as probably at the period of King Arthur's campaigns against the Saxon invaders, carried on early in the sixth century. Judging by their names, two of his battles, the eighth and ninth, may be located in the district of Cunningham, --one at Carwinnin, a fortress in Dalry, and the other at Carlung in West Kilbride. The tenth battle, that of Tribruit or Trathreuroit, has a name which corresponds so remarkably with one of our island-names as to warrant us, apparently, in identifying with Trawharry on the Cumbrae shore!

Another century from the death of king Arthur- who, indeed, according to the legend never dies-would see the lofty, self-denying labours of Columba and Kentigern brought to a close; the triumph of King Oswald, saint and martyr, who brought Aidan from Iona to teach his benighted subjects the doctrines of grace; and would also witness the entrance upon their evangelising efforts of the noble-hearted Christian ladies, Beya and Maura.

To these lady-missionaries-probably connected with families of princely rank-the whole of the West, to all appearance, from St. Bees to the Cumbraes, owed much. Their devotion to the religious instruction of the maidens who were taught in the schools ; their zenna-like operations in bringing gospel truth to bear apon the lives of the matrons who dwelt in the province they made their special care ; these and other agencies or social organisations, due to their activity and intelligence, brought the blessing that maketh rich to many a home. Did the Cumbrae church become a prey to the destroyer in any one of the wars that raged between Bretwald and Pict, then was it that Maura may have come to the rescue and provided the means for its complete restoration.

At any rate we know that Maura, after many years of self-denying effort in the best of causes, settled down in the island for good and devoted herself to the godly training of a company of young maidens. In the Creang-Haque, or hospice of the lady, did she pursue her duties, and when at times she visited her like-minded sister Beya (who spent the latter portion of her life in seclusion on Little Cumbrae), she brought away the cream of their discourse on spiritual themes, and imparted the whole of it to the promising young scions that sat at her feet and eagerly received it from her lips.

Little wonder if the grateful people among whom she dwelt called the name of the church which she loved to frequent by the honoured name of Maura, and so left to us of to-day not only the heritage of her bright example, but also the treasured name of Kil-Maura, now Cumbrae, or the church of Maura.

"Lady, that in the prime of earliest youth
Wisely hast shunn'd the broad way and the green,
And with those few art eminently seen,
That labour up the hill of heavenly truth,
The better part with Mary and with Ruth
Chosen thou hast; . . . . .

Thy care is fix'd, and zealously attends
To fill thy odorous lamp with deeds of light
And hope that reaps not shame."--Milton.

To reach Kirktoun and the site of the ancient church in the old churchyard, let the visitor pass up Cardiff- street, and straight along the road by the side of the mill-burn. Millburn House is on the left, a few paces in advance brings one to the Bowling Greens on the right, Maclellans-yards* are on the left between the road and the brook, and to the west of these are Sannoc-fauld, or field of the holy maid, and Feilcolm-knowe, or the knoll of the festival of St. Columba.

Nether Kirktoun is the farm-house on the left, and them fine field on the right is the Dawglon (good meadow), being part of the farm-lands of Pammachrey (right)--a name which appears to denote the residence of the chiefs of the clergy. Kirktoun farm-house is the one on the left, and the farm-road which leads from it to Portathro passes along the side of the field called Creang-haque. Keeping, however, by the main road we pass under the nine tall saugh-trees by the streamlet, and in half a minute reach the gateway of the ancient churchyard of Cumbrae. Patie's yard is right opposite the churchyard gate, and on the east side of the road. To the north by east of this "yard" are the pretty green hills called the

Shighans, or mounts of the fairy-folk ; and at the distance of a furlong right east from the same "yard" is the Corsfield with the Cors-burn, the rivulet of which falls into the sea at Covans-creek.

The Bell-man's yard lay between the churchyard and the manse avenue, and Baillie's yard lay next to the gate of the churchyard, being on the right as one enters the cemetery. Besides these yards, or garden plots, there were in close neighbourhood a good many more yards and cottages, all of them mying on the west side of the burn, and constituting in the aggregate the old clachan or kirk-toun.

Before we enter the churchyard a few more localities may be briefly noticed. Play-hill is about north of the Shighans, and the Lausy-hill, or hill of the blazing fire, comes next. In this hill the fairies, according to report, used to "roast their ham," the smell of which was sensibly felt by peasants passing that way! Clanypott, or abbot's meadow, lies north-west of the Fairy-mounts, and this meadow is bounded on the west by the syke or rivulet of Lagalein. Glastran- fauld, or the glebe-land of the (sainted) lady, may be found by walking a distance of ninety yards from the manse gate northwards, and identifying it with the field on the right or east side of the road. This very ancient glebe probably embraced all the land traversed by the road in this quarter, but the full elucidation of the point would detain us too long. Suffice to say that Keill-croft and Port-gelsie Park lie west of the road, and both of them are on the north side of the parisg minister's manse. The latter of these two local names is properly written Prot-gelsie, and evidently signifies penance-kirk ; but see Landmarks, p 83, for an alternative redering, viz., Lady- kirk.

Pennance-hill is in the north-west side of the manse garden, and quite near to it. A perforated rock on the hillock marks the spot where apparently an ancient church, cell, or chapel stood. Certain of the old inhabitants of the island have a tradition that "the Romans," that is, the Roman Catholics, did penance here. Probably an image of the founder of the chapel was fixed to the perforated rock. prot-ghelsey was evidently the old name of the place or chapel.

Entering the churchyard, the site of the old parish church (pulled down 49 years ago) will be found at a distance of about 33 yards nearly due west of the entrance or lich-gate. The tombstone of the Rev. Henry Graham, who died in 1798, was placed very near the south wall of the church, but outside of it. As this stone--a --"throch" one--has not been shifted, it serves as a "methe" or mark whereby to determine the former position of the sacred edifice. This church was built in 1802, and it stood upon the same site as that of the church built of "fine hewn stone" in 1612, which latter church replaced "ane kirk callit Sanct Colmis Kirke," or the church of St. Columba.

The next entry on the record connects this same church with the "chapel of Cumray" granted in 1318 by Walter the Steward to the monks and abbot of Paisley. this is not stated in so many terms in the deed of gift, but it is made certain by the Confirmation thereof, a few years afterwards, by the Bishop of Glasgow.

A long period of blackness--five centuries of it-- precedes this reference to the gift of the church, and brings us to the beginning of the ninth century, at which time the fierce Norwegian invaders burned and destroyed so many churches in the West. About this same time the record of the succession of abbots of Kingarth suddenly ceases, caused, we cannot doubt, by the ravages of those northern pirates and slayers, who harried and burned Iona in 802, and four years afterwards slew sixty-eight of the monastic family there.

Cumbrae church was only too likely to receive the hostile attentions of the hardy but destructive sea- rovers, and it is to this period of violence we must assign the building of the refuge-hold on the Lorne. Whether this "dwelling of strength" proved sufficient for the defence of the churchmen and their flock cannot be told, but the memory of the noble stand they made against ruthless foes was cherished by succeeding generations, and handed over to our keeping to-day in the beautiful name of Kennara Borough, or the fort of the Christian teachers.

Glancing back still farther, we find that the Chapel-on-Island of the Virgins was built in the year 714, and as this chapel is evidently none other than Chapel Santa Vey (St. Bey's memorial chapel) in Little Cumbrae, we take the testimony of early chronicles, the breviary of of Aberdeen and certain other facts and conclude that the church of Maura was built within the walls of this grave-yard, or near vicinity, some years prior to the death of King Oswald in 642.

It is a long time to look back to, but the reader is assured that the date just assigned is approximately correct. Now, as Beya and Maura were so closely associated in their lives and good deeds, so also in death they were not long divided.

Maura died first, her end having come at the place called Kilmavvris in the Breviary. Kilmaurs, in Ayrshire, has been imagined to be the place where Maura breathed her last, but it is much more likely that the Cumbraes witnessed the devotion of her last hours--l'ultimo sospiro. Beya died shortly afterwards (Nov. 3--her anniversary), and was buried in that Isle of Cumbrae wherein she spent the evening of her days, and in that same island a chapel of graceful design was erected in her honour. This chapel became the resort of pilgrims, whose pious aspirations were fostered and quickened by the remembrance of her godly example.

Cumbrae Church may not have been inscribed to the memory of Maura until early in the eighth century. After having been so "inscribed" the church would be called after her Keil-Maura, shortened into Cumbrae [kum'ra] by elision of the letter l-- a common occurrence in old names, e.g., --Kilcaiss or --Kincase.

Kilmaura, in Ayrshire, is locally pronounced kimmaurs. That the ancient Cumbrae Church became the subject of a double dedication need not be doubted, for such double dedications are far from being uncommon. We may, therefore, trust Dean Monro (writing in 1594) when he tells us that there was a church in the island called St. Colm's, and his statement is borne out by the local name of Feilcolm Knowe.

Maura must have been honoured at Whitinghame, East Lothian, for there are lands at Papple, in that parish, which are still called by her name--" Terre de Popill vulgariter vocate Sanct Mawris landis inconstabularia de Hadington."--Lib. Respons., cited Kalendars of Scottish Saints, s.v. Maura. Nov. 3.

Probably she had some connection with the ancient ecclesiastical establishment at Papple, one of the considerable importance in former times. A small part of the ruins still remains near the present farmhouse, and increase greatly the value of the state.

Did space permit something might be said about the worthy ministers who, since 1626, have attended to the spiritual interests of the islanders. In that year the Rev. Thomas Moore was parish minister, and he is the first of the Reformation ministers whose names are on record. Moore has, up to the present date, had eighteen successors, the present incumbent being the Rev. James S. Macnab, who was ordained to the charge of the parish in 1867.

Nearly a century ago the Rev. James Adam, A.M., was ordained to the charge, and he died in his eighty-third year after a ministry of more than thirty-one years. He was a good kind man, and when a beggar came to his door he used to make him repeat the commandments, and if the beggar proved capable of the task he was counted a respectable person and duly entitled to the silver coin which the minister gave to all such. It is reported that, in his church services, he was wont to pray for the "Big and the Wee Cumbraes, and for the adjacent islands of Great Britain and Ireland !" Some have affected to doubt the authenticity of the story, but it is certain that the traditionary report is of a piece with the well-known idiosyncrasies of the old pastor.

Like not a few other preachers of his time, Mr. Adam was accustomed to use the Scottish tongue in his pulpit ministrations, saying, for example,-- "an' Saura leuch" (and Sarah laughted.) Now and again he would finish up am earnest exhortation to his little flock by saying, "My friens, let us a' learn tae dae weel ; let us dae gude and be gude, and gude 'ill come o' us."

Quite recently the parish church has undergone extensive alterations and repairs, and it is now said by competent judges that the sacred edifice, internally, is one of the most beautiful and chaste on the west coast.

CHAPTER IV

LITTLE CUMBRAE

LITTLE Cumbrae may be reached by boat from the larger island in about twenty minutes. Sheannawally Point, or the point of the old cairns, is the name of the little headland which lies nearest to the pier of Millport. The distance by water from this "point of the old cairns" to the Auld Castle is not much more than a mile. It is now evident that the islet on which this old castle stands was formerly called Allinturail, that is, the islet of the noble's tower. Cravies-hole, or the creek of the devout folk, is at the north end of castle-island, and it is, at high water, a fairly good landing-place. But boats very often put in at the strand beside the farmhouse, and this is best managed when the tide is within two hours of reaching high-water mark. In order to visit

SANTA VEY,

the ruined chapel of St. Bey (Latine Beya), let the traveller turn round the farmhouse, keeping to the right, and proceed due north to the old ruined barn under the cliff called Craigmillar; then still northwards for three hundred yards; after that, bend round sharply to the left while traversing a pass at the north end of the line of cliffs and advancing west by south towards Priest-hoy—a beaked or wedge-shaped cliff crowned with some stone wall, on the right. Turning now slightly to the right and "doubling" the point of the cliff, let him advance about eighty yards westwards and he will presently find himself by the side of the ruined walls of Chapel Santa Vey, having traversed from the sea-shore rather less than a mile of ground, but doing it all easily (though partly up-hill) in half-an-hour.

This very ancient chapel has been planted in the green, fern-clad hollow of a rocky amphitheatre, the craggy ridges and cliffs of which completely shut off the prospect beyond, and confine the view to a mere bit of blue sky. Meet habitation for a hermit it is, and if ever the fashion of going into retreat pure and simple comes round again, we may feel sure that the green solitude of Santa Vey will be one of the first to invite the ascetic's choice.

Here, if anywhere, the solitary would find himself at home, for "in this calm spot remote from men" there is nothing to awaken the echoes from the cliff but the scream of the plover, as she rises from the covert of the reedy lake. It is just such a place as meets the requirements of the legend of St. Bey, and so far as this goes it affords internal evidence of its truth. Turning now to the chapel ruin we find that it had been a little fane 42 feet in exterior length, 20 feet of which belonged to the choir or channel. The choir was 20 feet in exterior width, and was divided internally into two sections so as to allow one of them to be used as a "prophet's chamber" or lodge for the priest in charge.

The ruined form or outline of this little sanctuary is about sixteen yards from the foot of Priest-hoy cliff on the right or north-east ; and the tiny, rush-tufted lake of Gurag Meyre, or the lady-lakelet, comes within a few paces of the west end of the chapel. About twelve yards south-west of the chapel there a couple of rifled grave-kists, which have evidently been constructed of rude stone slabs after the manner of ancient, pre-Christian interments.

Whether one of these formed the last resting-place of St. Bey, or is to be regarded as a pre-historic tomb of much earlier date it were hard to decide ; but this may be said that even Christians of conservative tendencies were not indisposed to adhere to the archaic mode of sepulture.

The larger of the two graves is about 7 feet in length, and lies east and west. The stone which forms its western end is a large block of porphyry 30 inches above the bottom of this "full-length cist of flagstones set on edge."

Since the breviary of Aberdeen does not say that the memorial chapel was raised over Beya's grave, we are tempted to think that this may have been the hallowed spot in which her ashes reposed. The other grave is within four or five feet of this one, lies about north and south, and shows a slab fixed in the earth, at the southern end of it. The little mere or lake (of the lady) is within three or four yards of this grave.

About eighty paces south by west of the chapel, and near to the rocky brow which overhangs the deep-lying lake of Langmere, are the ruins of a very old house of considerable size and strength, it being 22 feet square. As this 'lerrock' or ruin is near an ivy- clad rock beside the precipice we may call it Ivy-crag ruin.

Passing onwards over a smooth rocky eminence somewhat like a bare scalp of rock, and now in a south-easterly direction, a short walk of fifty paces brings one to another ruin about 30 feet in length, in the eastern corner of which stands the stump or butt- end of a round tower, most probably one of the kind so often found associated with ancient churches and (according to Dr. Petrie) used as bell-towers, some of them built as early as the middle of the seventh century. This round tower stands due south of the chapel, and may thus be quickly reached by the aid of a compass. Sometimes the writer has been ready to regard it as a square tower about ten feet square externally, but whatever its exact form it was probably used as a bell-tower. Anyone standing near the chapel can, in clear calm weather, distinctly hear the striking of the hours on the clocks of the parish church and the cathedral, in the Greater Cumbrae, although the latter church is about 2½ miles distant as the crow flies. The fact was proved in the personal experience of the writer, who along with his brother stood on the spot referred to on the afternoon of Dec. 9, 1872.

One of these ruined buildings may have been used long ago as a hospice for the reception of pilgrims visiting the shrine of St. Bey. No ancient slab-crosses such as those on Sanda island, Cantyre, have been heard in connection with the chapel which has been engaging out attention.

The South Chapel.-Walk from the supposed round tower for about ninety yards in a north-east direction and come upon the ruins of what has probably been another chapel—one of perhaps later date. It lies very nearly due south of the conspicuous southern point of Priest-hoy, from which it is distant fifty-five paces. Indeed, that high nib or point is like an index finger pointing straight to this ruined chapel, for such (by the testimony of competent judges) we must conclude it to be. And since no name has hitherto been found for it, it is now suggested that it be called Markle, that is, the chapel-ruin. As to length and breadth it seems to have been the almost exact counterpart of Santa Vey, and may possibly have been a reproduction of the latter upon a fresh site. Markle has good lime cement in its walls, one of which (the north) is three feet thick, and is still well seen. The priest in charge had a pretty large house or chamber attached to the north wall of the choir, but outside of it.

The remains of this chamber show it had an interior area of about 18 feet by 10. Close to the north wall of this exterior dwelling there is a squared block of sandstone fixed in the earth, while all round no rock but hard trap or clink-stone (of which the chapel is built) can be found. A little way north a cairn may be seen, and not far from it the site of an ancient homestead.

The Bel Stane.—Going southwards from Markle, a short walk of 96 paces brings one to this interesting stone, where the games and sports (devotions being over) were held on the festival of the saint. Approaching it from the chapel, this great stone shows the form of a finely pointed pyramids five feet in height. It rests on a bare patch of rock surrounded by greensward and bracken. Seven paces to the right, or due west of it, will be seen what may be called the Cup Stane, because of the cup-like hollow on the centre of its south face. this stone has the form of a hemisphere, with cup sculptured on its "plane" face looking towards the true south, the diameter of which face is 3 feet 3 inches, that of the "cup" 4 inches, and the depth of the latter nearly 1½ inches.

A work of man's art it is, but its meaning or purpose remains a mystery. Not so with the Bel Stane, for no tool has been lifted upon it, and its name it certainly has from the old term bel, buil, billie, a festival, feast, play. These two stones form a combination that is unique, and have attracted savants from distant places. Banclan-toye, or holy-woman's hillock, is one-third of a mile to the north of these stones, and may be seen on the right bank of a rivulet which runs westwards.

The name evidently refers to St. Beya of this island, who was honoured with a church at Dunbar, (Bae's Well is there,) another church at Kilbucho, and a third at Kilbagie. Besides these, there is reason to believe that the ruined chapel of Kilbaig in the Lewis was named after our lady-saint, whose day is the same as that of Maura. When the name of St. Bey has cill [keel] prefixed, it is pronounced Vey by the Gaels.

Here are a few verses which the writer lately penned in illustration of the ancient chapel of St. Bey:—

SANTA VEY.

Far up among the rocky heights and scars
Which stud the rugged breast of Cumbrae's Isle—
Erst called 'of Santa Vey,' but 'Lesser' now—
One spot of sweetest green attracts the eye
And bids the wanderer pause. For all about
Rise terraced steeps and craggy walls of trap
Which make of it a quiet sanctuary,
And shut one off completely from the world.
A calm retreat in ancient times it was
When good St. Beya chose it for her cell,
And made it hallowed ground for evermore.
A tiny lakelet here called Gurack Mere,
Whose straightest English is the Lady Lake,
Reflects the grassy verdure of its rim
And shows, in its clear mirror, chapel walls
Which dwellers on the isle call Santa Vey.
A shrine it seems within a natural shrine
To which the pious folk did oft repair
With reverence due to Him who framed this wild—
As for a lodge in lonely wilderness—
And with a grateful feeling in their hearts
Towards that good lady who, for many years,
Did teach with zealous mind and kindest love
Their daughters and their wives throughout the West.

143

The blest Evangel was her daily theme,
And well may we believe that many hearts
Received th' engrafted word which quickly grew
And proved to be those goodly plants of grace
Which, watered by the dews divine, bear fruit,
Some thirty, sixty, or an hundred-fold.
Strong time has laid its finger hard upon
The crumbling remnants of this little church
Which for a thousand years or more has borne
The shock of tempests and the blows of fate.
For long before the hardy Norsemen came
In gallant ships which raven-pennant bore
And deeply scored the billows of the Clyde,
Our sainted Beya and her close-knit friend,
St. Maura of the greater Cumbrae's Isle,
Had taught together in their mission schools
Those holy truths which tell us 'God is love.'
No mere recluses they in earlier years,
But ever active heralds of the Cross,
And making all their influence deeply felt
From high St. Bees to fair Kilmaurs in Kyle
As well as in the Isle of Cumbrae hight.
Now after years of labour thus were spent
St. Bey resolved to seek seclusion deep
Within the lone recesses of that isle
Where relics of her chapel still remain.
In perfect calm and meditative mood
She daily sought by prayer and fastings oft
To win that crown of truest sanctity
Which evermore grew fairer to her faith.
To none free access to her isle was given,

Save only to her friend of former days,
That faithful Maura, who did often claim
One hour's brief converse on some sacred theme.
Of these two friends the latter went before,
And soon thereafter to her rest was called
The venerable Beya, whose remains
In that same isle were decently interred.
Forthwith a chapel in her honour rose
And pious pilgrims to it came in troops,
As if the sight of their old teacher's grave
Would quicken their devotions, and create
A sense of joyous comfort in their prayers.
So with the circling years the custom grew
To have some play or game on our saint's day,
And, strange to tell, the Belstane on the green,
not many roods away, remains to mark
The chosen scene of their high festival,
Where possibly the feat of miracle-play
Was oft performed ; and afterwards the games
And minor sports which please the laic heart.

Cravies-hole, or creek of the devout folk, is
beside the old castle, and shows the spot where
the pilgrims landed. Monks Cave is two-thirds of a
mile south of the old castle, and will be found at
the base of the lofty cliff of Storrils—a cliff, which
is on the west side of the lower part of Cosey-
glen, the glen of caves.

This cave of the old monks or "Reimkennars" (Culdee clerics or hermits) is over one hundred feet in length, and quite dry. The entrance to the cave is effected through a deep rift in the cliff, and is somewhat difficult to discover.

Secure within its hidden recesses (where are high ledges to sleep on), the peapar or clerical fathers of Santa Vey must have often lodged here in evil times or when violence was feared. The polished smoothness of the sides of this cave is held to indicate the frequent inhabitation of it. There are several other caves in the vicinity, and there is also a pretty large one at Waterloo-bight called Ryssel-cave, or cave of the champions.

Ocregman's Cave, or cave of the bedesman, must be mentioned, if it were only for the opportunity it gives of interpreting a very remarkable name. The name of this old hermit bedesman's cave is formed by adding the common term "man" to a Gaelic compound signifying the cave of the man of prayer—uagh fhir ghuidhe.

The Magga-clagh [claff] Cairns on the northern point of this "Little Isle" are clearly shown by their name to have been the reputed burying-place of Picts. When the largest of these cairns was opened in 1813, the Earl of Eglinton's men came first upon a sword of great length and weight, and having a guard for the wielder's hand ; next, a hauberk of scale armour with iron byrnie or breast-piece, and iron guards for the wrist and back of neck. An iron casque or helmet was found along with these ; also a second sword so corroded by rust that it fell to pieces directly it was touched. Going farther down into the cairn the workmen came upon a short kistvaen, or chest of stone slabs, in which was found an urn, containing some brown dust and four or six fine white teeth.

The two swords and the other pieces of armour belonged to one or more secondary interments, but the cinerary urn must be referred to some ancient chief of the Gadini or the Firbolgs (see Landmarks pp. 117, 299). The Mariners' Chart, by an error of the press gives the name under consideration in the form of Muggie-point, but Magga-clagh is the only proper spelling.

Sheannawally is the name most frequently applied to the great cairns just described, and which are well worth a visit (Compare Magga-law in next chapter.) There are vestiges of a fort on the cliff-top a short distance south of these cairns. Millar-fort, a very old ruined stronghold, is on the hill to the west of the farmhouse, and its vestiges may be seen near the north margin of a small lake— Tammis-loch.

THE AULD CASTLE was built prior to the year 1375, for in the spring of that year King Robert II. made it his place of abode for a season. The fact is proved by a charter which the king, in the midst of his hunting and fishing expeditions, found time to seal and authenticate by the royal sign manual.

Again, in the spring of 1384, the king is sojourning in the same island, and from his royal residence there dates another charter. Perhaps the castle was built by his father, Sir Walter, the High Steward, who married Marjory Bruce the only daughter of the patriot king. In that case, he is the nobleman referred to in the name of Allinturail.

What a pity that the Bishop of St. Andrew's, or other churchman attending the king's insular Court, did not indite a little book, telling us all about the hunting, and the eagles, and the hermits, and the old chapels on the isle. During the period of the king's visits, and for long afterwards, Hunter of Hunterston was custodian of the island and its lordly castle.

Cromwell's soldiers are reported to have surprised and burned the castle in the year 1653,—an act of revenge, probably, for having confined in the dungeon of the old keep, and afterwards hanged, Archie Hamilton, one of the Protector's chief correspondents.

"On his [Cromwell's] arrival in Glasgow, 'the ministers and magistrates flee all away. I got to the Isle of Cumbrae with my Lady Montgomery, but left all my family and goods to Cromwell's courtesy, which indeed was great." —Baillie's Letters, iii., 29, cited by Hill Burton.

The Light-house should be visited, and the whole of the truly romantic scenery near Bolls Rock explored. Barr Hoy is the highest summit, and on one of its western ridges is the Whistling Stane. let him who hears the whistle try to solve the mystery of it!

CHAPTER V

WEMYSS BAY, LARGS, AND FAIRLIE.

ALTHOUGH our available space is now so limited, we shall do our best to turn what we have to good account.

WEMYSS BAY is in the west of the county of Renfrew, a name which signifies the rath or fortified town of the chiefs. Vanduara, or town of the giant- heroes, was in much earlier times a place of strength, and may have been either at the county town or in the wood of Durchat, near Paisley. It is a piece of mere hardihood to say that this town of the mighty heroes was a Roman camp.

We should rather adhere to the view which makes it a stronghold of the Downans, a Firbolg race, who may have had something to do with Downies-hill, near Castlesemple. Agricola, or some of the generals who came after him, may have visited these parts, and built bridges and roads, but we must bear in mind that Dunrod, or the hill of the fort, and many other strong places within the country, were held by the Celtic lords of the district for generations prior to the coming of the Roman cohorts.

One of these strong places is the Torr of Meagle, or the hill of the stranger chiefs, and this is the very "place of strength" which has proved to be the source of the name Skelmorlie, the meaning of which is given at p.106. A stronghold of note it had been, and was probably held for a time by some of those Fomorian pirates and sea-rovers, who infested the coasts of Britain during the period of the Roman occupancy, and who were, for the most part, men of Teutonic race. To connect such a famous site with those fancies and fables which represent it as the scene of serpent-worship and the theatre of demonical orgies, is simply to discredit the plain testimony of obvious facts, and to produce a downright caricature.

Some years ago the writer of these pages carefully examined the site of the above ruined burg, and also two more of Mr. Phene's so-called "serpent mounds." The result was a complete demolition of the philosopher's craze, in the despatch of which effective aid was given by a company of the best Scottish antiquities. It is, therefore, much to be regretted that a theory so vain and flimsy—not worth powder and shot—should be reproduced in the pages of any local Guide-Book.

Wemyss Bay has its name from the "weems" or caves which sea- waves, in the course of a long past geological epoch, have worn in the face of the shore line of cliffs. Pretty caves they are, and quite a home for the tufted fronds of the shiny-green harts- tongue and other ferns.

Had they been only a little larger and deeper we should, perhaps, have had amongst them a Monks' cave as in Cumbrae, or a Jerrygaha (giant's cave) as in Kintyre. But indeed, the "halyman" or hermit could not be far off, for a little way in the rear stood the "chapel of penitence" (see p. 106).

Here some local critic may say that the writer has not got the proper form of Annat-yards, and may mentally proceed to correct him. If any such does so challenge anything in regard to this matter, let it be said that Timothy Pont is the writer's guide, followed up by a searching study of the old local names?

And yet in such a matter as the interpreting of old names of places we find sciolists rashly venturing in where wise men fear to tread. It is an entire reversal and discrediting of the inductive method—that candid and patient questioning of the witnesses to which, in many of the sciences, we owe so much. Does the name Skelmorlie really have that meaning which the present writer, says it has? Undoubtedly so. Well then, are we to believe the author of any "brochure" Guide to this locality when he says that "auchen" signifies a field, that "clachan" means a stone circle, and next, a church, that Irvine is the greywater, and that Cumbrae has its name from a Gaelic word signifying "fragrant?" Certainly not. We must bow out of court these and all such erroneous conclusions.

IRVINE, as a name, simply means the water-side, clachan is a stone-house, and hence a chapel. Kempock, as a name, has nothing to do with "a maiden," but is simply a appellation for the grave of some gallant sea-roving captain from the northern strand,—the name being a pure Norse compound signifying the champion's cairn. The greater part of this cairn has disappeared, but the spot is marked by a great rude pillar-stone (see Landmarks, p. 32).

As a corrective of many errors in this matter of the interpreting of local names, let it be briefly stated here that the attempts which G. Chalmers, in his Caledonia, made to explain many names of places, do not merely bear the stamp of half-knowledge, but of so much less as to make them more of a hindrance than a help to the young student of philology. Portrye is explained at page 20, and must have had its name long before King Hakon bade his men row him ashore in order to have a mass said. Caves and dens are called "weems," even, when earth-houses are not meant. Dunoon is the heroes' fort, Rothesay is the castle-islet, and is a Norse name, as the present writer has been the first show. Daff-glen has its name from the Celtic word daimh, a church, and the fact favours the alleged antiquity of "Auld Kirk. " Spango means the steep hill-side water, and the Kip is the hill- head brook, as coming from an upland ridge.

Wemyss Bay is a bracing sea-side resort, and numerous handsome villas testify to its popularity. From any station on the Caledonian Railway it is easily reached, and a well- organised service of steamboats enables passengers to find ready access to many of the other watering-places on the shores of the Firth. It has several churches, and a first-class Hydropathic Establishment. Numerous fine villas and residences skirt the shore in front of the picturesque cliffs of Skelmorlie, and a still larger number occupy favourable sites on the higher grounds.

Turning to the left, on leaving the Railway Terminus, one has Kelly Glen on the right, the lands of which were long held by the Bannatynes. A walk of half-a-mile brings one to the fine pebbly strand of the "White Wick" of Wemyss (wick, a little bay), near to which is the Post Office.

Passing along the Bay, the visitor has several handsome villa residences on the right, and presently comes upon a fine succession of highly picturesque cliffs. Ferncliff sits snugly under the red crags, which find fit adornment in fern and flower and tree. To the north of this villa is the English Episcopal Church, a beautiful Gothic erection, built, A.D. 1879 in memory of the late Mrs. George Burns, and containing a memorial window in honour of the late Earl of Shaftesbury.

In the near vicinity is WEMYSS HOUSE, the residence of Mr. George Burns, proprietor of the estate of Wemyss Bay.

A little farther to the north a noble pile of buildings arrests the eye and engages the high admiration of the beholder. This is CASTLE WEMYSS, the residence of Mr. John Burns, Chairman of the Cunard Company. It is a handsome castellated edifice of imposing dimensions and commanding position, and has been justly described as "a rare and striking specimen of the old Scottish baronial style."

The fien red sandstone used in its construction receives the full effect of the harmony produced by its lovely environment of green lawns and shrubs and terraces.

Within the Castle grounds there are numerous and extensive conservatories, vineries, and peach-houses; a Lawn-tennis ground available for four courts ; a private pier of solid stone masonry, from which to board Mr. Burns's

magnificent steam yacht "Capercailzie," R.Y. S., of five hundred tons—at anchor in the offing,—these and other accessories of a large establishment combine to make Castle Wemyss a remarkable illustrations of the happy results of well- directed taste and enterprise.

LARGS.—The prescribed limits of this little book deman a severe curtailing of this section ; but, as such an attractive watering-place as Largs has long proved deserves better treatment, we hope to see soon a Hand-book to this locality which shall be worthy of its many interesting sites. Largs has its name from the Gaelic learg, a green slope, a hill slope, a sloping country-side. There is such a "Largs" or Larg-hill at Straiton, and there is another in country near Oban.

The meaning is certain, and it must be noted that the idea or notion of "a pass" is not associated with the term. A green slope may, indeed, be mounted, but beyond that there is no definite conception of a pass connected with the term learg.

According to the above Largs was originally the name of the sloping countryside in its vicinity, and was subsequently transferred or applied to the hamlet which sprung up around the ancient church of St. Columba. Magga or Meaga Law was a cairn of vast size which stood for ages in a field about one hundred yards north of Haylie. This cairn has been removed, and only the gigantic kistvaen or chest of stones remains. Its name has an evident connection with the Meatae or Picts, and it shows that, in olden times, this cairn was held to belong to people of that race.

157

One of its names, when interpreted, points it out as the tomb of a Celtic lord. Margets- law is another (a corrupt) form of its proper name. Hadil [haddil] is a name for it (O.S.A.), and this signifies the site or place of the grave-mound. Haylie is a name which denotes the mansion-house slope, and has nothing in the world to do with "helle, a pit or burial-place."

Gilburn is near at hand, in the vicinity of which Pont places Killinocraig, or the wood of the crag. The same old choreographer, writing nearly three centuries ago, places hereabouts the name of Paddoc Kirddin, or the camp of the Picts.

Kephanburn, meaning chapel-burn, is at the near end of Fairlie. Trigonie, judging by the camp at another place of the same name, should denote the heroes' fort or fenced town.

Greeto or Gritow has its name from the numerous stones of its channel, —griot-a', river of stones, or small boulders. Greta, at Keswick, is the same.

Gogo also is of Norse origin, and signifies the moss- land water. Fichen is a green plot or stripe of pasture, Firret of Keith is the moor-land of sheep-folds. Ringanros is tho robbers' cairn, and Camyir is the high kame or ridge between the counties. The "Deid Man" is at Coukilreeva, or the mossy-hilt fold.

The old folks in Lochwinnoch used to say (when the wind was in the north),—"It'll be fine weather to-day, for t'wind's aff the Coukils," that is, the quaghills of Misty-law and Hill o' Staik, —Norse stac, a towering mass of rock, a peak. Kempis-riggs are the champions' allotments of land, and Aghanvranchan (castle- hill) denotes the stronghold of the Fomorians or sea-rovers.

Noddisdale has certainly got its name from the camp or fort called Castle-law in Aitken's map. Netslie contains the same Kymric word for a fort, viz., naid, and this is confirmed by the Laverock-castle near Kilburn. Laverock is laurach, meaning the site of a ruined fort or building. Raillies keeps in mind the ancient reilig or cemetery near Chapelton and the Dokeers of Pont's time.

These places (a rich and lovely region) are on Kelsoland, or the land of the house of prayer— an extremely early church. For Aplenira (Aplas) see Landmarks p. 130 ; but if Applehirst be the true name of the place, then hirst, bush, copsewood.

Eddelyburn is in this quarter, and the first part of the compound signifies the site of the peel or stone tower,—aite ailigh. These details (though dry enough) may be useful to some inquirers.

FAIRLIE.—The charms of this delightful sea-side resort are well known. It is certain that great numbers of Northmen settled on the islands and shores of the Clyde firth. They were men of a noble race, and were often called firdar in their own tongue, meaning strong men, "warriors". Hence the name of Fairlie, or its older form Fairnelie, signifying the heroes' camp or settlement.

Such original settlements, were, of course, protected by a bulwark of earth called "birren," or by a stockade of heavy timber. Redding is in the neighbourhood of the village, and signifies camp, a fort. This may have been the strong place of the early fair-haired settlers. Fairlie Castle may have, in a later age, taken the place of the primitive stronghold.

Chapel- house, an old local name, explains itself. But the name of another chapel at Southannan is not so obvious. It is, however, known by old records to be St. Anan's Chapel, that is, the chapel of St Adamnan, the biographer of Columba.

The whole of this charming sea-board is a pleasant place to dwell in, and in taking leave of it so early we can only do so, in the hope of returning soon to its sunny shores.

[End]

Readers Notes:

Printed in Great Britain
by Amazon

83352144R00098